# FRAGMENTED GEOGRAPHIES

## A SHORT CRITICAL ANTHOLOGY OF JEWISH WOMEN'S WRITING IN THE BALKANS AND LATIN AMERICA

This book is dedicated to the memory
of Marjorie Agosín (1955–2025):

*Mentora, hermana, amiga.*

# Fragmented Geographies

## A Short Critical Anthology of Jewish Women's Writing in the Balkans and Latin America

*Edited by*
Oana Hergenröther, Marjorie Agosín,
and Jelena Filipović

Solis Press

© 2025 Solis Press and the
contributors, see page 104

*Cover artwork:* Michal Held Delaroza, "Fragmented Geographies," 2023. The mosaic is reconstructed from the parts of a broken hand-made ceramic dish, whose rearrangement does not aim at concealing the fractures between them, but at creating a whole made of pieces of histories, narratives and memories – a process that echoes the gathering of voices that are forming this book. The Hebrew word חי (*Cahi*, Alive) is written on the back of the black pebble painted with the turquoise Tree of Life. The fact that it cannot be seen reflects the idea that a hidden, secret source of life exists inside the fragmentary.

*Images on pages i and xxvii:* Michael Arroyo.

Published in 2025 by Solis Press.

All rights reserved. No part of this publication may be reproduced, stored in a retrieval system, or transmitted, in any form or by any means, electronic, mechanical, photocopying, recording or otherwise, except as permitted by the UK Copyright, Designs and Patents Act 1988, without the prior permission of the publisher. The authors of this work have asserted their rights under the Copyright, Design and Patents Act 1988 to be identified as the authors of this work.

This book is sold subject to the condition that it shall not, by way or trade or otherwise, be lent, resold, hired out or otherwise circulated without the publisher's prior consent in any form of binding or cover other than in which it is published and without a similar condition including this condition being imposed on the subsequent purchaser.

ISBN: 978-1-910146-97-2 (paperback)
ISBN: 978-1-910146-98-9 (hardback)

Published by Solis Press, England
*Web*: www.solispress.com | *X*: @SolisPress

# Contents

*Editors' Introduction* . . . . . . . . . . . . . . . . . . . . . . . *vi*

Part I: The Scents of Memories

May You Make a Good Bride (excerpt) . . . . . . . . 2
    *Rosa Nissán*

Windmill . . . . . . . . . . . . . . . . . . . . . . . . . . . . . . . 10
    *Myriam Moscona*

The Scent of Rain in the Balkans (excerpt) . . . . . . 12
    *Gordana Kuić*

Farewell . . . . . . . . . . . . . . . . . . . . . . . . . . . . . . . 17
    *Ava Kadishson Schieber*

Remembering Silivri at the Hotel Majestic . . . . . . 26
    *Ruth Behar*

In Search of Marie J . . . . . . . . . . . . . . . . . . . . . . 30
    *Michèle Sarde*

Sarajevo Underground . . . . . . . . . . . . . . . . . . . . 35
    *Andrea Jeftanovic*

The Portuguese Synagogue . . . . . . . . . . . . . . . . . 51
    *Angelina Muñiz Huberman*

Part II: In Search of a Lost World

Jerusalem Is a City on a Hill . . . . . . . . . . . . . . . . 60
    *Mimoza Erebara*

Prisoners *and* Old People's House . . . . . . . . . . . 61
    *Luljeta Lleshanaku*

Amidah: The Silent Prayer . . . . . . . . . . . . . . . . . 63
    *Entela Kasi*

Silence *and* Pretty Salonican Girls . . . . . . . . . . . 64
    *Rita Gabbai-Simantov*

Part III: What Our Grandmothers Knew

It All Started in My Grandparents' Pantry . . . . . . 66
    *Jelena Filipović*

In the End What Remains Are the Words:
"A Late Letter to My Grandmother Sali" . . . . . . 83
    *Michal Held Delaroza*

*Editors and Contributors* . . . . . . . . . . . . . . . . . . 96

*Copyright* . . . . . . . . . . . . . . . . . . . . . . . . . . . . *104*

# Editors' Introduction

## *Love, Loss, and Life between the Biobío and the Danubio*

> "The women of our family will come to me in dreams at night and say:
> Modestly we carried a pure blood across generations,
> Bringing it to you like well-guarded wine from the cellars
> Of our kosher hearts."
> Kadya Molodowsky (translated by Kathryn Hellerstein)

> "Today I am convinced that the journal was what allowed me to survive. For the rest of my life, it has also been a way to survive that *survival*, which is a less obvious problem."
> Ana Novac on her concentration camp journal
> *The Beautiful Days of My Youth* (translated by George L. Newman)

The space we seek to open up in this book is only partly geographical: that is why this editors' introduction evokes a physical stretch of land, sea, mountain, marsh, desert, and woods, between the two rivers, Biobío originating in the Chilean Andes and flowing into the Pacific at Concepción, Chile, and the Danube, running through various countries in Central and Southeastern Europe and letting the Black Sea embrace it in Romania. The space between the two rivers is vast, but not as vast as the spiritual sweep of thought and creativity that we want to bring to the fore. This anthology moves freely in and between space and time, chasing answers to the questions we pose: where do the Biobío and the Danube flow into each other? What songs, in verse and prose, do they sing upon their meeting? What is the nature of their touch? Who are the Jewish women writers who direct the flow of these two rivers, easily, almost playfully, making them merge, tangle, and pour into one another to the point of indistinguishable cohabitation?

Latin America and the Balkans have several trains of thought that make the parallel between them not only possible, but logical: first of all, their marginal, ex-centric position in relation to their far more powerful neighbors – North America and Western Europe, respectively – has very often made them into repositories of narratives of Othering, but it has also given them privileged positions of observations from the fringes. Within Latin America, negotiations of identity have taken place in every single of its regions and nation states owing to the complicated legacy of colonial past, immigrants from all over the world, diverse power structures fighting for a say; owing to a great diversity of heritages in terms of high linguistic diversity (severely endangered in some places), cultural niches, vast geographical spaces, economic inequality. Within Europe, the Balkans, though a much smaller geographical stretch, have also been a place of historical encounters, a place where cultures have co-lived and co-created for centuries, often sharing a common language and a common destiny, while also separating from this common destiny violently, as we have witnessed in the fracture of the former Yugoslavia in the 1990s. A second, and for us most important parallel, is that both Latin America and the Balkans have, over the centuries, been extremely important places of Jewish sanctuary. The two regions also notably share a geography of refuge and a Jewish geography of the world that continues to redefine and reimagine itself. In the south of Chile, for instance, in the heart of the Araucanian territory, a small community originating from Monastir (now Bitola in North Macedonia), in the then-Ottoman Empire,[1] arrived and settled, creating a Sephardic school and a burial society. Gabriela Mistral, the Nobel Laurate, taught in this community in Chile (where Pablo Neruda visited her in his teenage years) and this was the place where Sephardic (and Jewish heritage more generally) grew

---

1  On the history and story of the Jewish community in Monastir/Bitola see, for example, Uri Oren's acclaimed 1971 novel *A Town Called Monastir* (translated from the Hebrew by Mark Segal), Dror Publications.

to become an increasingly important plain of self-identification for Mistral. A second example is from the present moment – showcasing, as it were, how the mirrorings of Jewish destinies in the two regions transcend space and time – namely, the recent feature film *Adentro mío estoy bailando: The Klezmer Project* (2023), which, through a hybrid, autofictional and metafictional form of Leandro Koch and Paloma Schachmann's extradiegetic love story, also tells the story of the search of two young Jewish-Argentinians for the(ir) roots of klezmer music throughout eastern Europe. Their journey takes them from Buenos Aires through and beyond Romania, Moldova, and Ukraine. The film was awarded the Best First Feature Award at the 2023 Berlinale[2] and intertwines the personal story with Yiddish traditions of klezmer music, the Latin American with the Southeast European, the personal and the communal, laying bare the connections that we, too, are trying to uncover in this book.

Creative voices which shape this anthology are neither harmonious nor act in unison: women of different ages, from two continents of complex ancestries, whose homelands (imagined and geographical) are all very much entwined with their Jewish ancestry (both Sephardic and Ashkenazi). Social contexts in which these extraordinary women are born into – different countries with intricate cultural tapestries, ravaged by wars and political turmoil, in which they still manage to find periods of tranquility and safety – have affected the way they express their identities across a number of literary genres.

In order to understand the selection of authors and their illustrative pieces of writing, it is necessary to understand the line of thought behind the methodology applied by the editors. First and foremost, the driving force underlying our search was to understand the process of personal identity construction in connection with social, historical, and cultural contexts on both diachronic (ethnic, religious, racial, etc.) and synchronic axes (gender, professional, national, transnational, etc.) in Jewish women from differ-

---

2  www.berlinale.de/en/2023/programme/202308143.html (accessed October 1, 2025).

ent geographic regions and different generations. In our search for socially constructed knowledge, we looked at narratives, i.e., discourses, "in which language is interpreted as the basis of all human existence, a cohesive force which imposes cultural patterns and limitations to our social and speech communities" (Filipović 2018, 19). Identities, as we see them, are not in any way exclusive (in terms of individual vs. collective entities), they are not simplified and described in "dichotomous terms as either micro or macro, individual or social, local or global, etc., with hyphenations allowing for a limited degree of complexity" (Blommaert 2015, 1–2). We see them as chronotopic, defined through "the intrinsic connectedness of temporal and spatial relationships that are artistically expressed in literature" (Bakhtin 1981, 84–5, cited in Blommaert 2015, 4).

Consequently, we view literature, which we have focused on, as an excellent resource to look deeper into the intentionality of meanings represented in literary works (Murphy 1978, 121, cited in Filipović 2014, 407), which at the same time provides us with a more thorough perception of the complexity of "interactions between practices and creativity in social life" (Blommaert 2015, 2) on the one hand, and artistic expression on the other. Moreover, we dare think that by designing this anthology, we have created a very specific type of space in which our Jewish female authors populate individualized places in accordance with their understanding of representational communicative practices, which are identified as "both the practices by which certain kinds of representations are brought into existence, and the practices by which those representations are used, shared, and manipulated" (Brewer and Dourish 2008, 9). Literary narratives in prose and verse are most certainly created with the objective to be "used, shared and manipulated" in a sense that they invite their reading audiences to engage in negotiation of meaning and interpretation.

The notions of space and place play a very significant role in the design of our artistic chronotopes, i.e., time–space configurations (Blommaert 2015). We view space as a dimension in which social phenomena are distributed. They are limited by social systems and their actors, and they possess their own internal structure (Filipović and Filipović 2015, according to Curtis and Jones 1998). Moreover, space is understood "as an area of freedom and mobility" (Yi-Fu, 1977, 54), a conceptual notion, a cognitive landscape which functions in terms of time–space configurations, "which are then translated into dialectical, dynamic and transformative meaningful complexes of peripheral and centralized semiotic elements (van Leeuwen 2005), socially, historically, temporally, and spatially conditioned, but at the same time, individualized and rooted in each person's worldview and cultural models of their communities" (Filipović & Vučo 2019, 349). The arrangement of time–space in this anthology, where space is delineated as the dimension through which aesthetic communicative occurrences are distributed, is a complex spatial system of concrete geographical locations on both diachronic and synchronic axes (which have shaped Jewish history over centuries) as well as a symbolic notion which involves agency in the creation of individualized places defined and presented through specific narrative patterns, performative expressions of identity relevant to each and every author's identity, without trying to categorize them by static and limiting criteria such as age, geographic location, ancestry, or literary genre.

Our authors in their writings give individualized shaping to their places by "enclosing and humanizing them" (Westphal 2011, 5), which some authors claim create "a calm center for established values" (Yi-Fu 1977, 54). In our case, however, the center is far from calm! The center of each writing entry in this anthology is filled by contradictions, doubts, disappointments, fears, hopes, and, in all cases, empathy and care.

In this anthology, different genres are to be found: fictional narratives based on personal life experiences – the excerpts from novels *Like a Bride* by Mexican Rosa Nissán, *The Scent of Rain in the Balkans* by Serbian Gordana Kuić, and "In Search of Marie J." by French-American Michèle Sarde; personal memoir narratives "Remembering Silivri at the Hotel Majestic" by Cuban Ruth Behar, "Farewell" by Serbian-US-Israeli Ava Kadishson Schieber; a multimodal text by the Balkan-Argentinian Andrea Jeftanovic, "Sarajevo Underground", together with "The Portuguese Synagogue" by Angelina Muñiz Huberman, and the short story "Windmill" by Myriam Moscona, both from Mexico; beside poems by Mimoza Erebara, Entela Kasi, and Luljeta Lleshanaku from Albania, and Rita Gabbai-Simantov from Greece. As heterogenous as they may appear at first glance, they all create a very well defined emotional and cognitive space, a "smooth space" which is coherent in spite of being "variable and polyvocal," a space whose places "unfold between points, [...] that can connect as many lines as one chooses" (Westphal 2018, 39).

Our selection and the writings themselves do not pretend to provide the audiences with generalized notions of historical, social, political, religious, or cultural frameworks of and in which they write. Rather, what constitutes the space and the places in this anthology are the authors' unique, singular, and authentic voices that open up windows with a clear view into their lives and the lives of their communities across time and space, thus helping us grasp how particular pieces of social and cultural knowledge are created and how they have shaped the authors' individual identities in relationship with those of different communities through which they move both physically and metaphorically throughout their lives.

* * *

Our work for this short critical anthology draws on previous collaborations, which happened in and between the United States, Austria, and Serbia. At the University of Graz in Austria, we engaged in two science-to-public events: in 2019, in "Imagined Landscapes. Jewish Women Writers in the America and the Balkans," an introduction that would have a continuation in the form of a bigger event in 2023, in the garden of an Art Nouveau villa belonging to the university, an event where Oana Hergenröther gave the framework and the floor to Marjorie Agosín and Jelena Filipović, who talked about "Unexpected Encounters: Jewish Women Artists from the Americas and the Balkans." And further, in the two special issues of *Nashim: A Journal of Jewish Women's Studies & Gender Issues* (Brandeis University Press/Schechter Institute of Jewish Studies in Jerusalem/ Indiana University Press), entitled *Writing Our Way Home: Jewish Women's Post-Holocaust Diasporic Writing in Latin America, the Balkans and the Jewish World* in the two thematic parts of which[3] we further explored the interconnections, the echoes, and reverberations of this phenomenon.

The voices in this anthology recite over very original geographies: Angelina Muñiz Huberman's family lived in Spain since the fourteenth century, emigrating eventually first to France and then to Mexico, where she would discover her Sephardic roots and become an important voice of Mexican Sephardic literature. Gordana Kuić lived her life as part of the small Belgrade Sephardic community, while drawing the inspiration for her most acclaimed work from the Sarajevo Sephardic roots in Sarajevo, especially her aunt, Laura Papo Bohoreta (famous for being the most renowned Sephardic woman writer of the Balkans from the first half of the twentieth century). Andrea Jeftanovic, a promising Chilean writer, begins to rethink her Bosnian and Bulgarian origins and explores the dualities and complementaries of the worlds of her Christian father from Bosnia and her Jewish-Bulgarian mother. In the work of Michal Held, her Sephardic ancestry from the city of Córdoba opens views of her father's heritage as a Romanian Jew, making her feel as a member of a Jewish Balkan community as well. What we want to achieve through these voices is the creation of intersecting maps and geographies that are fluid and imaginative. For it is the writer herself that defines through her texts how (her) identity and (her) politics merge.

\* \* \*

One of the most politically-pregnant aspects of any identity is – language. Speaking, writing, and identifying with multiple languages

---

3  *Part I: Surviving Stories* (Number 39/Fall 5782/2021), and *Part II: Imagined Landscapes: Jewish Women Writers between Worlds* (Number 40, Fall 5782/2022).

has always played a crucial role in the formation of complex identities of artists who create multi-sensual worlds using words. The significance of language as phenomenon is thus contradictory: on the one hand, we can say that the depth of imagination transcends any discrete language – and on the other, we can acknowledge the importance that language plays, precisely because, as broadly as its arms can reach, there are always limits to the breadth of this embrace. All the more, then, are the insights we get from and by plurilingual and pluricultural writers crucial for our understanding of loss, life, and love, as the title of this critical introduction says.

The extraterritorial character of Ladino or Yiddish, for example, has meant a life in parallel imaginaries: a writer was/is both Jewish and Israeli, and Romanian, Polish, Greek; she is also, like authors in this book, both Chilean and Bosnian, like Andrea Jeftanovic; or Cuban and Turkish, like Ruth Behar; or Romanian and American like Nina Cassian, etc. To exemplify the multi-locality character of Jewish writing over time, Shmuel Refael writes, for example, about the complexities of Ladino writers throughout the nineteenth and twentieth centuries (in what is today the nation state of Greece) saying that it "served as a liaison between the various geographies and territories in which the Sephardim lived. Life in an extra-territorial and suprageographic space continued until the terrible Holocaust" (Refael 2012, 323–4). The deep faith in humanity, the belief that one can and indeed should strive to be more than one thing in more than one place, is also something that many of the texts in this book evoke.

Many of the texts, however, especially coming from writers whose Jewish families settled in Latin America, continue to deal with the loss of those languages now turned a misty, nostalgic magic: many of them speak no Ladino, no Yiddish, and/or none of the local languages their families had known in Europe and the Middle East (Bosnian/Croatian/Serbian, Farsi, Hungarian, Portuguese, Romanian, Turkish, etc.). Andrea Jeftanovic, born to a Serbian Orthodox father and a Jewish-Bulgarian mother, regrets not having been taught any of the languages that paint the broader picture of her family history, on both sides; she remembers these languages (Serbian, Ladino, Bulgarian), as the languages of adults, of secrecy, of problems to be kept away from children (see Cerdán 2011). Ilan Stavans, in his introduction to the English translation of Rosa Nissán's novel *Like a Bride* mentions this language loss in clear terms referring to both Nissán and her Jewish-Mexican writer-compatriot, Myriam Moscona:

> Moscona and Nissán, as Sephardic Jews from Mexico, came of age listening to [Ladino]. The jargon appears somewhat prominently in Nissán's oeuvre, especially in *Like a Bride*. Curiously, it is not heard from the mouth of Nissán's protagonist, Oshinica, but by those in her entourage, most of them immigrants from Turkey and, prior even, from Persia. (2002, xi)

The secretive, almost exotic taste of these languages, therefore, signifies both love and loss for the authors (and, often, protagonists in their work); it also very often signifies a prompt to seek out and search for what was lost, and often find unexpected treasures, if not the ones the author/protagonist had envisioned.

* * *

The forces of historical and lived reality, the individual fates and faiths, the "hats" women poets took on and their identities that ran parallel to their artistic selves – mothers, daughters, granddaughters, daughters-in-law, professionals – made both them and the texts they created into a unique force of creative imagination. Throughout the two regions – Latin America and the Balkans – women writers, over time and space, produced texts; just like their texts, in turn, repeatedly produced and transformed who they were. They drew from their Jewish origin, but they also drew from the socio-economic reality of the time they lived through, from the social milieu they were born into, from the brutal interruptions of verities they were used to: in the form of fascism or Stalinism, for example. An interview with the Ladino scholar Ivana Vučina Simović in Part III of this anthology takes the reader through a personal account of a discovery of family secrets and hidden lineages that influence the scholar's career, but also her transformed sense of proximity to the topics she has dealt with from a distance. The political becoming personal, and the personal being understood as political are complex processes that science and creativity alike have been trying to understand anew in different socio-historical realities – and these realities, in turn, shaped the understanding itself.

Jewish women writers often had to face the decision of nurturing what the Yugoslav-Jewish Hungarian-speaking author Judita Šalgo calls "careful identity" (Šalgo quoted in: Dražić 467-8). Šalgo herself, born in 1941 in Novi Sad, then Yugoslavia, now Serbia, was taken by her biological mother to a Serbian woman in 1944 and was told to address the woman as "mother" from now on: it was this necessary deceit that saved her life and that, certainly, added complicated layers of trauma and self-identification, in terms of origin, language, and belonging, all more than present throughout this writer's work and activism until her death in 1996. In claiming her "careful identity," the author sublimates and resumes her experience of perpetual instability originating in the shattering of "this primary relationship in life, the relationship between mother and child"; out of it "grew her consciousness of the replaceability of everything that exists in this world, including herself" (Dražić 468).

The trope of silence permeates, as widely known and researched, the history of Jewish thought and art. Ruth Behar (born in 1956), in this anthology, says, concluding her text about her mixed, and partially lost, Sephardic and Ashkenazic heritage: "I will continue on my journey, moving beyond the silences of the fathers, to find the words to speak of a community that has made the remembrance of loss the core of its spiritual quest." These many silences are, for the author, a combination of respect, feelings of loss and resentment, and a very specific kind of reverence; born in Cuba and having lived in the United States since she was a child, Behar brings in her text a juxtaposition of two geographical points that can seemingly be no further apart: Silivri, in Turkey, and South Beach, Miami. But the two, as we read, can simultaneously be no closer to each other. The French author Michèle Sarde (born in 1939), herself only self-defining as Jewish at a late point in life, calls this phenomenon in her essay "the crossing of silence." It is a silence, made deeper by the passing of decades, that her family needs to keep, but which the author herself decides to break, in a search for a grandmother she is always told to be the spitting image of. Angelina Muñiz Huberman (born in 1936) describes here a moment of reflection in a quiet synagogue, a silence that the text almost makes us hear. Herself a character in a complicated history of leaving, fleeing, returning, she has explored in her texts the complex feeling of a parallel connection and disconnection from the events of World War II, and perhaps the most poignant phrase in the text this book brings is recognizing the silence of the Portuguese synagogue in Amsterdam for what it is: "a monument to the divine absence." Like many other places of lost presence, like Lublin or Thessaloniki, the narrator finds it difficult to relate the conspicuous absence of Jewish life with the monumentality of a once live and lived place of worship. Coming from across the Atlantic, but having been born in the south of France (after having been expelled from Spain at the time of the Spanish Civil War), and having landed first in Cuba, then Mexico, and having eventually studied in the United States, Muñiz Huberman's encounter with the memory of place of Anne Frank and Etty Hillesum positions her as a third, silent and brooding analyst of the two girls' approach to the presentiment of hell they both expressed in their war diaries.

For many Jewish women who wrote and write in languages and cultures and worlds of a majority culture, there is perhaps a less overt connection to Jewish life, their Jewish roots and Jewishness. But it is through themes such as violence, oppression, the struggle of women, motherhood, feelings of dejection in face of cruelty, that they express what they have learned, heard sung and read to them, what they inherited as part of their Jewish identity. In Slovenia, Berta Bojetu-Boeta (1946-1997), daughter of Jewish-Slovenian Partisan parents, wrote novels and poetry about dystopian universes where women are terrorized, kept in the dark and forcibly attacked, violated and then performed abortions on, women who recreate, painfully, the bits that were shattered in and for them. Sexuality, a central issue and the means of subjugation, was questioned and analyzed by this feminist author in a time when her country – the Socialist Federative Republic of Yugoslavia in the 1990s – was being shattered to pieces from within, and where rape, alongside abandonment, poverty, hunger, and fear, was reality for many women off the page. "The beauty of Bojetu's prose," writes Metka Zupančič, "lies in the inner strength, especially of her female characters, to stay focused in the eye of the storm, to persevere, to create safeguards for love and collective growth, for friendship and trust, which can in time prepare the ground for different human relationships" (Zupančič 2004, 281). Berta Bojetu travelled to Jerusalem with her son, working there on the novel *Birdhouse (Ptičja hiša)*, for which she went on to win, as the first woman author, the Kresnik award, the most important literary award in Slovenia. This came, however, after Bojetu-Boeta had published her two novels in Austria, rather than her home country; in the south-Austrian province of Carinthia, a region with a large Slovenian-speaking population, publishing houses were more open towards the experimental and non-conventional and published other writers who did not find a home in Slovenian publishing. "That she was published within the Slovenian minority culture in Austria, and not in her home city of Ljubljana, reveals the uneasiness with which Bojetu's home country, even post-1991 independent Slovenia, regarded the work of this unconventional woman" (Zupančič 2004, 282).

Unconventionality, riskiness, daring, is perhaps more a necessity than an exception in the careers of authors living with more than one language.

Ana Novac/Novák, the pen name of Zimra Harsányi (1929–2010), "now a forgotten writer" (Petrescu 140), is an author whose multiple identity layers swathe her, like sheets, in a mystery worthy of being found in literature itself. "Novac's life story is worth knowing because it showcases the tragic fate of an East European Jew during the twentieth century, when first nationalism and fascism and later Communism uprooted and almost decimated the Jewish community in Transylvania" says the author that tries, in a text, to reconstruct Novac's life based on her file with the *Securitatea*, the

Romanian secret police (141). This complex personality, a Jew born into a Hungarian-speaking family in Romania's north, fled to France in the 1960s and became famous for her memoir from Auschwitz, Płaszów, and six other camps, *The Beautiful Days of My Youth*. Novac's introduction to the English edition of this book, which she revised several times, opens with a clever, concise, insightful, and poignantly funny description of her "origins," that perfectly captures the complexity of belonging, of roots, of the multiculturality that was and is woven into the core of Southeastern Europe, and which, precisely, the Nazi ideology (but also others before and after) sought to fight, against all odds, against:

> I was born in Transylvania, a region that three peoples – Romanian, Hungarian, and German – have argued over in three languages for centuries. That is why, except for an accident of birth (the fact that I am Jewish) I have never been able to specify precisely either my nationality or my native language. I came into the world under a fascist dictatorship, spent my youth under a communist dictatorship, and between the two, for a change of pace, I did a tour at Auschwitz and seven other concentration camps.
>
> When I was born, on June 21, 1929, at Dej, in northern Transylvania, that town was Romanian. At the beginning of the war, the part of Transylvania where we lived became Hungarian once again, then Romanian again after the war. In three generations my family changed nationality four times. (Novac 1997, 3)

Novac is occasionally called "a Romanian Anne Frank," which might be slightly misleading, as her own diary, as one author points out, started where Anne Frank's stopped: inside the camps (cf. Bohus 2023). Over the course of her imprisonment, she used "camouflage paper, [...] posters saying WORK WILL MAKE YOU FREE; CLEANLINESS IS HEALTH, and other things, which I pulled off the walls and cut up to make sheets" (Novac 7). She hid the scraps of paper in shoes, hers and of others willing to help her, and salvaged the papers that were to become a book out of the camps. The physical struggle of the author, the tactile dynamics between the words and the writing surface are one of those literary tropes and sources of literary anecdotes that never cease to fascinate: from Mikhail Bakhtin who allegedly tore up the sheets of his manuscript for *Bildungsroman* to roll cigarettes during the war in Russia; to Alicia Kozameh, the Argentinian-Jewish writer who did the opposite, and while imprisoned for her activism against the Argentinian military dictatorship in the 1970s, used the cigarette paper she was allowed in her cell – for writing. Paper, that omnipresent surface of creation, has been used, over space and time, as a material tool for resistance.

Long after the war and the camps, Ana Novac discovered the heaps of paper, having chosen to forget about them until then: "a lasting amnesia that [...] allowed me to live out my youth, complete my education [...] and become an actress and then a playwright" (10). The book has appeared, in more or less edited versions, in many languages – English, German, Italian, Dutch, Romanian. Novac saw great success in her post-war years in Romania, where her plays in the socialist-realist style were performed in the country and abroad in other socialist countries (notably Hungary and the Soviet Union), until her fall from Communist grace and subsequent emigration, first to Germany and then to France.

The initial favor and subsequent disfavor of the state forces was to be the fate of Nina Cassian (1924–2014), another Jewish-Romanian writer. Born into a Jewish family in the important Danube port city of Galați, near the three-country border between Romania, Moldova, and Ukraine, a city with large Jewish, Greek, Lipovan, and Turkish communities, Cassian grew with and around intellectuals, her father translating into Romanian Edgar Allan Poe, Hans Christian Andersen, and classical German poetry. By the early 1980s, she had published over 50 books of poetry, literature for children, nonfiction, fiction and translations, including those of Shakespeare, Paul Celan, and Bertoldt Brecht. Besides her literary career, she was also an accomplished pianist and composer. And then, a break happened. In 1985, she traveled as a visiting professor for creative writing to New York University on a Soros Foundation fellowship, and while she was there, the Romanian *Securitatea* found written evidence of her anti-regime sentiments. Fearing for her life, she was granted asylum in the United States. Her apartment in Bucharest, meanwhile, was confiscated, her books banned and taken out of Romanian libraries and bookshops. It stayed this way until the Romanian revolution and the fall of communism in 1989. In the United States, however, she had to reinvent, both herself and her career: like Ana Novac, who had reinvented herself writing in Hungarian, then Romanian, and then French, Cassian – over 60 years old at this point – switched from writing in Romanian and started publishing in English, in *The New Yorker*, the *Atlantic Monthly* and in 1998, a first book of poems written in English, *Take My Word for It*, where she wonders "Can I lose my doom, my limit, / the skin, tight as a straightjacket, of my native language?" and claims: "compared with my struggle with English / Hercules was a honeychild". (Cassian 1998, 45). The volatility and broad spectrum of Nina Cassian's poetry has been repeatedly noted: the persistent topics – love, rejection, loneliness, beauty standards, abandonment, passion, sex, embodiment, finality – inform the sensory presence of strength in her verses. Everything is physical and, as such, everything is painful, even love itself; and everything is lovely, even pain itself. There is a ripping-apart quality of duality, of mixing into explosiveness, as she writes about the "small," individual topics, and alludes to, touches on, gives us a smell and touch of those "big" historical ones.

Rita Gabbai-Simantov's (born in 1935) two short poems speak of that lost locus of Jewish life in the Balkans: Thessaloniki, or Salonica. Gabbai-Simantov is known for her poetry and other activities in Ladino, and these two short poems express two opposing forces that dominate Greek Ladino post-Holocaust experience: a remembrance of vitality on the one hand, and loud silence on the other. The local identity of Salonicans was so strong, Mark Mazower writes in *Salonica, City of Ghosts*, that, asked for their nationality in the 1920, Jews, Muslims, Orthodox Greeks, and all the other residents of the city would say that their nationality was – Salonican (Mazower 2006: Chapter 21: Greeks and Jews).

Ava Kadishson Schieber (1926–2022) is an author who embodies many of the lines of thought and destiny that we are trying to cover within our research on the present topic: her birth, her hiding in Serbia during the war, her subsequent life in Israel, but also her later life, reinvented, in the United States, her plurilingualism, and her ability to transform and adapt, all depict the uniting strands that we followed in choosing authors for this collection. During World War II, hiding in a Serbian family in the countryside was nowhere near simplicity: as many have noted, one had to change both the rough strokes and the details, from accents and vocabulary to rubbing the hands raw so they look like the hands of someone doing hard manual labor, instead of those of middle-class city Jews, among whom she had grown up. As Joel Halpern puts it in an interview for the Wexler Oral History Project conducted by The Yiddish Book Center in Amherst, "first off, [...] we have to make you look like peasants. So, unfortunately, out come the gold teeth, out comes the fancy bridgework, because this would be spotted by soldiers if they ever came" (Halpern 2023). Loss, therefore, voluntary or involuntary, has been part of the writings of the women artists present in this volume, in one form or another, throughout their careers. The already mentioned loss of that primary identification – the mother–child mirroring – that Judita Šalgo lived through and always reworked in her texts; the loss of distinctive language speech characteristics that might put one in danger, like for Kadishson Schieber; the loss of a diacritic, like in Andrea Jeftanovic's case ("c" at the end of her last name, instead of the original south Slavic "ć"): "It must signify something to lose that accent," Jeftanovic tells us in her text in this book, *Sarajevo Underground*.

What does it mean? Where do we situate loss? And where does the lost go? For some, it gets replaced, recontextualized: oak and walnut trees become palm trees; the Dinaric Mountains become the Andes; Adriatic Islands become Caribbean ones. For some, the loss means a permanent empty space, not to be filled by anything else. For others, the empty space has always been there, and it craves a lining, for its rough edges scrape at one's consciousness continuously. Such is the case with the Latin American writers in this anthology who go back to their families' roots in Southeastern Europe to understand not only communal, ethnic, and personal histories, but also to understand the region as it is today. Andrea Jeftanovic (born in 1970) makes the journey to the city and the country about which she has heard since childhood, which lives inside her bloodstream, but which, alas, exists no more once she has finally gone to it – after the 1990s war in Yugoslavia and the infamous Sarajevo siege. For the author, Sarajevo has always lived inside Santiago de Chile, and vice versa:

> the Drina and the Miljacka, rivers which became blurred with the Mapocho River and became navigable. Or rather, the stroll down Maršala Tita Avenue, which merged with Bernardo O'Higgins Boulevard, wide pathways in which there was traffic both ways. Saint Sava, the familiar patron of Serbia, appears descending from the Andes Mountains and stands in the middle of the monument to the war of Chacabuco. [...] Sarajevo became present each time I accompanied my father to the Russian Orthodox Church at the intersection of Holanda and Doctor Johow in Ñuñoa, a neighborhood in Santiago.

It is, then, possible, and indeed, a quotidian reality, to embody two regions that could seem so different, yet the loss (in this case, the loss of language) still can occur easily and irrevocably, as mentioned before.

Sarajevo is the site of Gordana Kuić's (1942–2023) successful series of novels telling the story, partly based on her own family history, of the Sephardic community in Sarajevo. Kuić comes from a tradition of Sephardic female creativity, being the niece of the famous Laura Papo Bohoreta, researcher and collector of Jewish folklore, feminist, and translator. Kuić finds inspiration in the story of her family, in the women of her mother's and Laura Papo's generation who, at the beginning of the twentieth century, with all its challenges, but also with all its new opportunities of modernism, were true pioneers of female social engagement. We can read Kuić's work (a successful and widely translated series of novels spanning stories from the nineteenth to the twenty-first century across the Balkans) as romanticized histories of the Balkans, as family sagas, as love stories, as historiographic metafiction. The chapter in this anthology tells about a moment of feverish change: the murder of Archduke Franz Ferdinand in Sarajevo in 1914, told from the perspective of a young girl.

An excerpt from the acclaimed novel by Rosa Nissán (born in 1939), *Like a Bride*, is also an intimate and repeatedly relatable coming-of-age story, made complex by the ethnic and religious constraints of a Mexico in the 1950s, a society changing, yet staying the same, which must have deeply perplexed the author herself, as the only partly hidden voice behind the narrator. It stands as reverberation here of Kuić's text before it, told, similarly, from a young person's point of view, taking in the complexities of history and the human nature creating it from a distance of inexperience.

We bring here a series of poems by three Albanian writers of different generations, Mimoza Erebara, Luljeta Lleshanaku, and Entela Kasi. Albania lived, over the twentieth century, periods of harsh segregation from the rest of the Balkan region, where many topics, including those of World War II, but also Jewish legacy and history on its territory in general, was under a veil of secrecy, twisted (hi)stories, and fear. Albania is a very different county today, but these three female authors touch on topics of silence and silencing – a quiet melancholia for what once has been and is lost permeating all the poems.

This anthology concludes with a text penned by Michal Held Delaroza. As literary scholars, we are united by a common curiosity. What is a text or a place that speaks about identity? Is identity shifting all the time and what is the relationship between memory and identity? In Michal Held's moving and inspiring essay, through the figure of her grandmother who lived in Romania and moved to Israel, she explores this theme, further forming her inquires through an eloquent poem about how and what we remember. Michal Held writes that we are united by words. And words are all that remains. Her grandmother was born into the Romanian language, but Michal's father, her son, refused to speak it. This concluding piece of poetry echoes other losses of linguistic heritage encountered in the volume. These fragments of memory of the

Balkans from a literary perspective, therefore, are the fragments of memory that every writer brings to her text – either through remembrance or through the acceptance of oblivion and the surpassing of it into a recreation of that which we only partly, and sometimes only instinctively, know. In this collection we explore the Balkans as a literary geography with multiple imagined possibilities. Romania is in many ways different to other Balkan countries but it has itself experienced many aspects of B/balkanization. Is Michal a Balkan granddaughter? This unanswered question is at the heart and at the end of our collection.

* * *

What seems to stand out among all the authors we have mentioned in this introduction is the ability to adapt; many of them after traumatic experiences, such as survival of death camps or oppressive regimes and exile; many of them in new professions, in new languages, reinventing themselves dynamically and constantly. Some of them in a state of post-memory, as Marianne Hirsch has called it, dreaming and fantasizing of an unpalpable world that they have been told they come from, yet living in a palpable reality thousands of kilometers and experiences away.

## Bibliography

Blommaert, Jan. "Chronotopic Identities. On the Timespace Organization of Who We Are." *Tilburg Papers in Culture Studies,* paper 144, 2015. Accessed on June 19, 2017. Available at: www.academia.edu/15207208/

Brewer, Johanna & Dourish, Paul. "Storied Spaces: Cultural Accounts of Mobility, Technology, and Environmental Knowing." *International Journal of Human-Computer Studies* 66(12), 2008. pp. 963–6.

Boase-Beier, Jean & de Vooght, Marian. *Poetry of the Holocaust. An Anthology.* Todmorden: Arc Publications, 2019.

Bohus, Kata. "Anne and Eva: Two Diaries, Two Holocaust Memories in Communist Hungary." *European Network of Remembrance and Solidarity,* April 20, 2017. Accessed on September 19, 2023. Available at: https://enrs.eu/article/anne-and-eva-two-diaries-two-holocaust-memories-in-communist-hungary

Cassian, Nina. "Invitation au voyage". In: *Take my Word for It*. New York: Norton, 1998. pp. 45.

Cerdán, Gianmarco Farfán. "Entrevistas desde Lima: Andrea Jeftanovic". December 21, 2011. Accessed on November 13, 2023. Available at: www.entrevistasdesdelima.blogspot.com

Cohen, Mark R. "The Origins of Sephardic Jewry in the Medieval Arab World". In: Zohar, Zion. *Sephardic and Mizrahi Jewry: From the Golden Age of Spain to Modern Times*. New York: New York University Press, 2005. pp. 23–39.

Curtis, Sarah & Jones, Ian Reese. 1998. "Is There a Place for Geography in the Analysis of Health Inequality?" *Sociology of Health & Illness*, 20(5). pp. 645–72.

Дражић, Силвиа. [Dražić, Silvia.] „Јудита сусреће Јудиту: ‚опрезни идентитет' кроз огледало критичког мимезиса (једно могуће читање)". *Зборник Матице српске за књижевност и језик* 2. pp. 467–81. Available at: www.ceeol.com/search/article-detail?id=689252

Filipović, Jelena. "Identity Construction through Discursive Practices and Code-switching in Autobiographic Fictional Narratives by Rosa Nissán and Gordana Kuić". In: Gudurić, Snežana (ed.). *Jezici i kulture u vremenu i prostoru 3*. Novi Sad: Filozofski fakultet Univerziteta u Novom Sadu, 2014. pp. 405–15.

Filipović, Jelena. *Moć reči. Ogledi iz kritičke sociolingvistike*. Beograd: Zadužbina Andrejević, 2018.

Филиповић, J. и Филиповић, J. [Filipović, J. and J. Filipović] „Простори, места и језици српске интелектуалне дијаспоре у сајберспејсу." *Српски језик од Вука до данас*, књига 1. Филолошко-уметнички факултет Универзитета у Крагујевцу, 2015. pp. 443–53.

Filipović, Jelena & Vučo, Julijana. "Multimodal Transdisciplinary Approach to Cultural Heritage Preservation. Linguistic and Cultural Landscapes." In: Gudurić, Snežana & Radić Bojanić, Biljana (eds.). *Jezici i kulture u vremenu i prostoru 8/2*. Novi Sad: Filozofski fakultet Univerziteta u Novom Sadu, 2019. pp. 347–57.

Halpern, Joel. "Sheltering a Jewish Family in Serbia". The Yiddish Book Center's Wexler Oral History Project. Accessed on: September 26, 2023. Available at: www.yiddishbookcenter.org/collections/oral-histories/excerpts/woh-ex-0000640/sheltering-jewish-family-serbia

Lieberman, Julia R. *Sephardi Family Life in the Early Modern Diaspora*. Waltham: Brandeis University Press, 2011.

Mazower, Mark. *Salonica, City of Ghosts*. New York: Vintage Books, 2006. E-book.

Molodowsky, Kadya. *Paper Ridges: Selected Poems*. In: Kathryn Hellerstein (ed.). Detroit: Wayne State University Press, 1999.

Nissán, Rosa. *Like a Bride; and Like a Mother*. Albuquerque: University of New Mexico Press, 2002.

Novac, Ana. *The Beautiful Days of My Youth*. New York: Henry Holt, 1997.

Petrescu, Corina L. "Of Sources and Files: The Making of the Securitate Target Ana Novac". In: Valentina Glajar, Alison Lewis, Corina L. Petrescu (eds.). *Cold War Spy Stories from Eastern Europe*. Lincoln: Potomac Books, 2019. pp. 137-59.

Refael, Shmuel. " 'Regaladas de sus madres': Judeo-Spanish Women's Poetry on the Holocaust". *European Judaism: A Journal for the New Europe*, 43/2, 2010. pp. 76-90.

Refael, Shmuel. "The Geography of Memory: The Representation of the Pre-Holocaust Salonican Jewish Community in Post-Holocaust Sephardic Poetry". *eHumanista* 20, 2012. pp. 321-33.

Smith, William Jay. "Introduction. Nina Cassian: Eight Poems." *The American Poetry Review*, Jan/Feb 1990, 19/1. pp. 23-5.

Stavans, Ilan. Introduction to *Like a Bride; and Like a Mother*. Albuquerque: University of New Mexico Press, 2002. pp. xi-xv.

van Leeuwen, Theo. *Introducing Social Semiotics*. London: Routledge, 2005.

Vučina Simović, Ivana & Mandić, Marija. „Orijentalno doba u kulturi sećanja Sefarda u Beogradu između dva svetska rata". *Antropologija* 19/3, 2019. pp. 113-43.

Westphal, Bertrand. *Geocriticism. Real and Fictional Spaces*. London: Palgrave Macmillan, 2011.

Yi-Fu, Tuan. *Space and Place: The Perspective of Experience*. Minneapolis: University of Minnesota Press, 1977.

Zimmels, Hirsch Jacob. *Ashkenazim and Sephardim: Their Relations, Differences and Problems as Reflected in the Rabbinical Responsa*. London: Oxford University Press, 1958.

Zupančič, Metka. "Berta Bojetu-Boeta's Feminist Dystopias". In: Cornis-Pope, Marcel & Neubauer, John (eds.). *History of the Literary Cultures of East-Central Europe: Types and Stereotypes*. Amsterdam/Philadelphia: John Benjamin, 2004. pp. 281-7.

# Part I

# The Scents of Memories

# May You Make a Good Bride (excerpt)

*Rosa Nissán*

## Second Grade

Every night I kneel down next to the window, gaze at a star (which is probably my guardian angel), and say the "Our Father" for God, and a "Hail Mary" for the Virgin Mother. Even though I'm the daughter of Jews, I hope that I have a guardian angel who follows me around all day long, just like my classmates have. Today I prayed that I won't have to change schools; they want to stick me in an elementary school with only Jewish kids. (Where do they get so many of them?)

> Dear Lord, make it so that I get to stay forever at Guadalupe Tepeyac Elementary. Don't let them take me out for anything in the world, especially now when I'm going to go into third grade—the most difficult year of primary school. Only here at this school, and with your help, will I be able to get through it. I promise you that I'll do whatever you ask of me: follow the Ten Commandments, go on Saturdays to catechism classes, and then, the day that I die I will be the guardian angel of whoever you say.
>
> In the name of the Father, the Son, and the Holy Spirit. Amen.

At eight o'clock in the morning, before beginning our studies, we always pray. We put the palms of our hands together near our mouths, we close our eyes, and then we all recite our prayer in unison. And Our Heavenly Father hears us. With our right hands we make the sign of the cross, and then we sit down to study. Our desks are really nice; the top lifts open and inside we store all of our school stuff. I have the top of my desk lid decorated with stickers: in the middle is Saint Theresa (I adore her), and on all four sides are other saints with flowers all around them. I spend all day giving them little kisses so that they watch over me.

When we complete our assignments or behave ourselves, the Misses reward us with another sticker. I'm one of the best behaved, and among those who have the most stickers. I just have to hide them when I'm at home because my mom doesn't like them very much. Sometimes she catches me making the sign of the cross in the morning. The other day she told me, "I would prefer it if you would leave the classroom when the others are saying their morning prayers." But I couldn't possibly do that. The rest of the kids would ask about me, and besides, I like saying prayers.

Yesterday during recess everybody was making sand castles. I was backing up to make mine a little bigger when I stepped on another girl's castle. She got so mad, and then threw sand in my eyes and screamed, "Jew girl, Jew girl!" Hearing that really surprised me, 'cause most of the girls don't even know that I'm Jewish.

A whole bunch more came around and then they started yelling "You people killed Christ!" and they made the sign of the cross in my face, and just stared at me like I was the Devil himself.

I yelled back, "That's a lie. I'm not a Jew. I say my prayers and make confession just like the rest of you."

It's almost one o'clock in the morning. I can't sleep. I keep thinking about how they threw sand at me.

* * *

This dream of Hell keeps haunting me. Last week I dreamed the same thing. The fire kept coming back to my bed to visit me, over and over. The yellow flames lit up the darkness, waves of orange and red fire. Then tombs opened up like manhole covers. People came out of them to walk toward God—he's going to reward or punish us. I can see the lids opening up, the resurrected people starting to walk. "The final judgment. We'll all be there someday," said Mother Mary. "Then we will know whether we'll make it to Heaven, or whether we'll end up with a tail and horns." The ones that go to Hell will make little kids do bad things.

* * *

Last night the neighbors came down from the second floor and we played Lottery. I got the playing card with "The Devil," and I lost because that old bad guy just never got called. That awful little red demon was dancing around with his evil eyes in my sleep last night. He's got this big iron fork that he uses to sweep the cinders around; he just comes and goes, wherever he wants. He gives me this look out of the corner of his eye, shows me his horns, and sharpens his talons on the burning edge of his blade. It just scares me to death to imagine that this could happen to me. Oh, I hope it doesn't come to that!

And why is it that we've got to go around naked? And with all those resurrected dead people no less! Oh, I would just die if they saw me naked, and if I then had to go out like that and have everybody see me. What an awful punishment! I'd run into all these people that died like a thousand years ago: Benito Juárez, Napoleón, Miguel Hidalgo y Costilla, my other grandma, Cinderella, Cuauhtémoc ... And how in the world is he going to be able to walk anyway, when they burned off his feet?[1] It must be that we come back all in one piece; they say nothing is impossible for God. It might actually be fun, if I get to meet all of these people, but ... naked? Oh, not that! How embarrassing! And without even anything to cover yourself up!

> Love God over everything else. (I love Him and I pray to Him.)
>
> Don't take the Lord's name in vain. (I'm not going to swear anymore. But if I do swear something that's not true, I'll cross my fingers behind my back, and it won't count.)
>
> Honor your father and mother.
>
> Keep the Sabbath and the Holy Days.

---

1  Benito Juárez (1806–72) was president of Mexico (1857–65, 1867–72), particularly revered as a champion of Mexican independence and democratic reform and as the first national leader of indigenous heritage. Miguel Hidalgo y Costilla (1753–1811) was a priest who led a rebellion against Spanish rule; he was eventually defeated and executed. Cuauhtémoc was the son of Moctezuma, who was emperor of the Aztecs when the conquistador Hernán Cortés arrived in Mexico in 1519. It is believed that Cortés's men tortured Cuauhtémoc by burning off his feet in an attempt to make him reveal the location of Aztec treasures.

Don't kill.

Don't fornicate. (This one I'm skipping. Who even knows what it means?)

Don't steal.

Don't bear false witness or lie. (I don't tell too many lies. Besides, it's the worst thing I could do to my mom.)

Don't desire someone else's wife. (I don't understand … whose wife?)

Don't covet someone else's belongings. (That's an easy one, 'cause I never want what isn't mine.)

If I just follow these, I'm sure I'll go to Heaven. The thing that I really like about the Ten Commandments is that they're the same for Jews and Catholics. Finally, something that's the same! I can recite them at home just like I can at school. At least I have that. It's easy to follow them, too, 'cause that business about me going to Hell is just too horrifying.

I want to go to Heaven and be an angel like on my stickers. I'd sure like to be one of the invisible ones. How fabulous to be invisible! Go everywhere, flying from here to there, seeing everybody without them seeing me … now if I could just get up close to kid's ears and tell them, "Don't pay any attention to the Devil! Give your Sundays over to the nice Old Man. Let other kids borrow your crayons, even if they break them." They say that the Devil comes and tells kids in their left ear to misbehave, and their guardian angel tells them in their right ear to behave themselves.

Those blond angels with the baby-blue robes and transparent wings live up in the sky and they get to see God, the Virgin Mother, and all the Saints, and talk to them. "Holy Cross, Holy Cross, make the Devil go away and Jesus come." Ol' pot-bellied demons—don't come around me—get out of here! Go away forever! I know that those little devils are really pushy and they keep coming back to your ear and saying, "Steal that pen, hit your sister, pull her braids, make fun of her!" Sometimes they convince you, because the Devil only teaches you bad habits, and those demons are very tricky.

My robes would be white; I'd fly around from here to there. I'd tell all the kids to be good, no matter what country they're from … but I'm not sure I'd want to be the angel of a Jewish kid, I'd rather have a Roman Catholic. Someday I'd take the highway up to the sky; I'd sprout beautiful wings like a butterfly, and from the clouds I'd throw buckets of water so that those below would feel like it was raining.

\* \* \*

All the girls at school get presents and parties twice a year; once on their birthday, and then on their Saint's day. But Jews don't get to celebrate the day of their Saint. The teacher asked me when was my Saint's day. The only thing that I could think of answering was that I would ask my mom. I'm sure there's no Saint Oshinica. I'll look in the calendar; if there's a Saint Eugenia, I'm saved.

\* \* \*

Since we live on Guadalupe Boulevard we get to see all the processions that come by every day toward the Basilica.[2] They go by singing and dancing and laughing; they drink arm in arm, carrying their children, their sick people, their food, their blankets. Each group has a guy in charge that watches out and makes sure that they don't go so slow that the procession behind catches up.

When we can just barely start to hear them, we run out to the balcony; we don't seem to ever get tired of watching them. Sometimes the groups are three or four blocks long, and when they pass us by, that's when it starts to get sad. But on the days close to the Holy Mother's day, they come by one after the other, bearing different standards, all with the image of the Virgin of Guadalupe—the Mother of all Mexicans—framed in threads of gold.

They must be having fun, coming from places like Toluca, Querétaro, Pachuca, and lots more. When they pass by our house they start singing "Mañanitas," so happy because they're about to

---

[2] The Basilica of the Virgin of Guadalupe, which sits atop a hill in Mexico City, is the nation's most famous cathedral, dedicated to its most beloved native saint. The faithful believe that it marks the spot where, in the sixteenth century, the Virgin Mary appeared to an indigenous peasant, Juan Diego, and requested his help in bringing his people to Christianity. It draws thousands of pilgrims each year.

get to the place where the Virgin of Guadalupe appeared for the first time. Many of them are so full of emotion just from being so close, their eyes fill with tears. Others are already on their knees, even though there are still fifteen blocks to go.

* * *

The whole area smells like *gorditas*. And all around the Basilica there are women sitting on their little steps off the street, warming up these corn tortillas on clay dishes. They're small, about the size of a quinto coin (well, maybe a little bigger), and come in packets of ten, wrapped in colored tissue paper.

I wonder why it is that they sell so many of those special candles all around down there. They're the really long and pretty rose-colored ones, and they're decorated with little golden flowers.

Sometimes we go inside the church to hear the mass. And sometimes we just walk around the vendor stands. Then we go up the little hill that you can just barely see from the window of our house. At the top there's a little white house with a cross on top. It's right there where the miracle happened to the Indian, Juan Diego. He sure was lucky! I hope that someday she can appear to me. If it's a miracle, then it could happen to me, too. Later on, we come down from the hill, and to get back home we take the train that goes all the way up Guadalupe Boulevard. That way we're not gone too long and Mom doesn't notice that we went down there again.

* * *

I believed them. I believed my parents when they said that it wasn't the Jews that killed Christ. "If they bother you again, tell them that Jesus was Jewish, that he made his Bar Mitzvah."

"Oh yeah, right, Dad," I said. "Like they're going to believe that! They'll just get mad."

* * *

Since my mom was to going to Monterrey to see my grandpa, Micaela hurried up with her chores and she took us down by the

Basilica again. We met up with some of her friends. After a while, I heard one of them say, "I'm telling you, Mica, you shouldn't be working for them. The money they pay you isn't enough—it runs out just like water."

I pretended not to hear this. The truth is, I don't know what to say when I hear that kind of talk. And then, what if they start in with the whole thing about killing Christ, too? Everybody must know about that. We went into the church on the hill and I just stared at the crucifix. Really, look how they left him! Some lady who was kneeling by us was crying 'cause he was dripping blood. That poor guy! How could you not hate whoever did that—what terrible people! It's been so many years since it happened, but you still have to feel awful about it. If this lady who's crying by me knew that I was a Jew, I really think she could kill me. The good thing is that Micaela likes me and she's not going to go around gossiping and telling on me. And besides, you can't tell if someone is Jewish just by looking at them. Frankly, I'm glad I'm Jewish rather than Black. But even I feel pretty sad and guilty about it. Look how they nailed him to that cross! What horrible people.

* * *

On the corner where we live there's a fine goods store, and the owners Berta and Bicha are friends of my mom. They live in the back of the store on the ground floor. They make the most beautifully decorated cakes. Sometimes I just sit for hours watching how they do one layer and then the next. They even make the little figurines, with paint and wires, then the flowers—different colors like blue, yellow, and pink. I think the prettiest ones are the wedding cakes. But I can change my mind when I see the ones to celebrate a *quinceañera*, with its little figurine coming down the steps of a circular staircase.[3] I spend a lot of time looking at them, and at the yellow, pink, and blue powdered sugar.

---

3   In Mexico and other Latin American countries, girls' fifteenth birthdays, or *quinceañera*, are marked with especially lavish celebrations that welcome them into adulthood.

Actually, the figurines don't look that great until we make them a little dress with a piece of tulle and attach it with a bit of frosting around the waist. Then we cover the pleats with the frosting from the decorating bag, and it looks just like a little waistband. That's when they really look elegant. Then we apply a little paint to make them dark or fair-skinned, and they end up looking just like we want them to. Poor things! But they're always pretty.

Bicha and Berta are friends with a priest who gives catechism classes on Saturdays at the church closest to my home. A lot of kids go there; we learn how to pray, and ever since I learned how to cross myself I'm better at knowing which is my right hand, 'cause it's the one you have to use to make the cross. When we're all done, they give us those licorice candies that I love so much. I've never missed a class because they cover for me and tell my mom that I'm with them helping decorate the cakes. I really want to make my first communion, and they're the only ones who can help me save myself from the final judgment; and even better, maybe God will forgive my whole family.

* * *

In our neighborhood, Colonia Industrial, there are a lot of other Jewish families; they've been my parents' closest friends since even before they were married. My mom introduced Max and his wife Fortuna. They've got kids, too, but I'm the oldest—we all get along great. Today my mom and some of the other ladies decided to go to a Jewish school that's over in another neighborhood, Colonia del Valle, to see if maybe all of us get together, the school will send a bus to pick us up. When we got home from school, we found out they had registered us.

## Third Grade

All of these kids killed Christ too? They seem all right to me. They don't seem like they could have done it. Maybe they don't remember doing it. They play marbles and tag and freeze tag—everything I played in the other school. Could they really be like my old friends? You can't tell at all that they're Jewish.

# Windmill

*Myriam Moscona*

In the main tent of the circus, the animal tamer lights a wheel on fire so that the tiger can jump through the circle of flames and land on the other side without getting burned. Two benches are arranged, one higher than the other. As in medieval rituals, the people beat their chests. There are men holding monoculars and women wearing hats covered in tulle. The tiger bypasses the obstacles with a grace that is recognized by the hundreds of spectators who scream with pleasure.

The tamer gestures that the final act will commence, and she introduces her head between the tiger's jaws. This is why I ask my father to carry me because I want to feel his arms embracing me in the rising tide of fear. Her luck running out, the tamer falls down on the ground with the tiger on her back … The scene continues: the tiger remains on the woman's back and is attacking her. An agitated and panting voice can be heard over the loudspeakers: "Ladies and gentlemen … a doctor, we urgently need a doctor! Can someone in the audience please help."

A river of blood begins to gush from one side of the woman's body. The tiger devours her. The people begin to swarm towards the exit doors, transforming into a violent mob. I don't know how much time passes. A confused sensation of fear floats in the air when an agitated yet falsely tranquil voice erupts from the loudspeakers once again: "Attention everyone. Ladies and gentlemen, the danger has been contained. The show will go on. Return to your seats. You are invited to go back to your places."

The tiger, having already smelled the blood, moves away from the body, its reddened snout beats against the canvas walls. The voice that requested calm speaks again: "Ladies and gentlemen, we cannot escape from our destiny. All of us are dead. Children, tamers, and beasts. All are dead."

I don't know what more the voice says. I cling to my father's legs so that we can leave the circus as soon as possible, and I feel the tiger closing in on me. I look up to ask him to carry me, but I quickly lose him in the crowd. Instead, I see my grandmother Victoria almost in front of me, and she very gently speaks to me: "Did you hear what they said? We are dead. No one is going to kill you because you are already dead."

—"Where is my father? I want to go with him."

—"Your father is in the chambers, my child, where they are burning the speaking tongues."

I don't know what she is talking about. From there I see the tamer, facedown and wrapped in a crimson cloud. There is no one left. The tiger, the people, my father, my grandmother, everyone has suddenly disappeared, except for me and the dead tamer. A voice deep inside says, "You are the last creature."

And then among the different girls who make up my being, the frighteoned one stands up, the one whose voice I hear more than I should. As usual, I place my hand on my throat to hear her speak.

Terror speaks inside with an altered voice like that of the *dibuk*, those spirits that are the souls of dead people who occupy the bodies of living beings, forcing the person who is possessed to behave as "other," and speaking through her in different voices.

The voice whispers to me in a raspy but high-pitched tone: "The things you run away from the most are the hardest to avoid."

And then I curl up next to the dead tamer, until I fall asleep.

# The Scent of Rain in the Balkans (excerpt)

*Gordana Kuić*

## Chapter I: Sarajevo, 1914

The next morning, as they were being washed and dressed to go out and see Franz Ferdinand's procession, Blanki listened in delight to Buka's story about the great Archduke who had come all the way from Vienna to visit them and how he would ride in with his wife in a big automobile with golden handles and with a whole cavalcade of generals in bright new uniforms, headed by Potiorek, the Governor General of Bosnia himself.

"Just look at the decorations, *ermanicas*," said Buka opening the window. "Little sisters, look: Sarajevo is preening herself today like a bride before her wedding!"

Indeed, Blanki had never seen this town of hers decked out so lavishly. Yellow and black flags of all sizes were fluttering in the breeze. As Buka tied her sisters' bows and fastened their shoe buckles, she told them how Bosnia had once been independent under its own king, until it was seized by the Turkish Sultan Mehmed II. After that it had belonged to the Turks for a long while, and then it was wrested from their hands by the Austrians.

We must be very precious if everyone's fighting over us, thought Blanki to herself, and then went on to say aloud: "You know what, Riki! I'll ask him for a bun and you can ask him for a dress!"

"*Buenu*, all right," answered Riki in agreement and added, "When I grow up, I'm going to marry a Jewish archduke and always have plenty of dresses and lots of buttered buns!"

"You cannot!" said Blanki sadly.

"Why not!? Why not!?" Riki protested.

"Because there are no Jewish archdukes."

"How inconvenient," Riki shrugged. "Then I'll have to find a rich merchant."

* * *

Blanki knew that this warm, hazy day, the twenty-eighth of June, was the date the Serbs of Sarajevo called St. Vitus's Day and celebrated as a great holiday. The Muslims, Jews and Catholics did not. It was a good thing for people to have different holidays, Blanki thought, because it evened things out and prevented confusion. If Serbs, Muslims and Catholics, for example, were to try to squash into the temple for Passover, there would be an awful crowd; and if, say, Jews, Serbs and Catholics celebrated Courban Bairam, then the mosque would be so jam-packed that people would have to queue up to wash their feet in the fountain; and what if the Muslims and Jews and Serbs were to go to Mass in the cathedral, or if Muslims and Jews and Catholics were to ... No, it would be impossible, especially because of the problem of space, which was the most difficult in the tiny Serbian church. Perhaps this was why, instead of going to church they celebrated their family's saint, Slavas, in their homes and the priests would come to them there to cut the Slava cake.

Blanki also knew that St. Vitus's Day was the sad anniversary of the Battle of Kosovo, when the Serbian King Lazar, way back in 1389, had lost to the Turks. It was little short of a miracle to Blanki that the Turks of Sarajevo, who were called Muslims as well as Bosnians like everybody else, spoke Serbian, the native language of their former enemies! And it was even more amazing to her that the Serbs consented to speak to them at all! Hadn't all those Serbs been killed by the Turks at Kosovo? Hadn't they been tortured and impaled on stakes? Hadn't their children been taken away as tribute to the Sultan? Perhaps lately they had decided to make peace, after they had counted up all the dead on both sides and discovered that the numbers were equal.

Blanki would have asked Buka about it on the spot, if Riki hadn't been fidgeting so much while Buka brushed her hair, and nagging her for a *kreutzer* to buy flowers to toss in front of Ferdinand. Her round cheeks were ruddier than usual, decided Blanki, looking at her own cheeks which were pale anyway, and even more so today. "It must be because we're so excited," she murmured to herself.

Finally, holding hands, with little Elias tucked safely between them, off the three of them went.

Blanki had never seen anything like it in her life: the streets were packed with people all dressed up in their best; it was like a sea of red fezzes, parasols, and broad-brimmed hats adorned with flowers. And every one of those hats was stitched together by her sisters Nina and Clara, thought Blanki with pride. How important they were! If it weren't for them there would be no milliner's shop, and if it weren't for the shop there'd be no hats, and if it weren't for the hats not a single woman would ever set foot outside her front door!

It was fabulous to stroll about a city with so many policemen, so many gleaming sabers, swords, scabbards and uniforms with braided epaulettes and polished buttons! Riki should marry a policeman rather than an archduke. But she wasn't sure if there was such a thing as a Jewish policeman. She would have to check.

The shallow River Miljacka gurgled and tinkled its accompaniment to the crowd's deep murmur as Blanki, Riki and Elias arrived at the Apel Quay.

Delightedly, Blanki peered over its stone parapets at the water rippling along, on and on, always in the same direction. What would happen if someone stopped it somehow and the waters began to rise? It could flood the whole city together with Tzar's Walkway, Chehaya Walkway, Latin Bridge, and Goat Bridge as well!

The white dazzle of all those bobbing parasols reminded Blanki of the soft, slippery carpet of fresh-fallen spring blossom that she so much loved to walk on. Ah, what indescribable beauty everywhere! She sighed deeply.

It was quite difficult to get through the tight circle of huge grown-ups, she thought, but she certainly couldn't miss the chance to go up to Ferdinand and give him her greetings.

"Everybody's taller than us!" exclaimed Riki furiously as she tried to squeeze between the splayed feet of a colossal gendarme, whose boots were planted like rocks in front of her. Her lips pouted, and an impish little smile flickered across her face. Blanki knew that she was up to something, so she called to her, "Riki! Come here! *Ven aqui!*", at which the gendarme shifted his stance, so Riki's piece of mischief collapsed.

"Is His Majesty coming this way?" Blanki asked the gendarme timidly, while Riki tugged at his sleeve and yelled at the top of her voice, "Where is he!? Where? Where? Tell me!"

"Hey, that's enough! Run along, kids!" retorted the policeman.

Although she couldn't see anything, Blanki suddenly heard a piercing shout. The crowd began shoving and jostling, hemming them in entirely. Then people started running. A terrifying noise was followed by an ominous silence. As the mass of bodies around her thinned, Blanki caught sight of a white skirt, with funny red markings spattered over it. "*Vamos de aqui, prestu!*" she cried in a frightened voice. "Let's get away from here!" She glanced at the faces of the grown-ups around her. She had always considered faces far more interesting to look at than animals or trees or sky. But now they scared her. Something was wrong here, very wrong. On every side she was surrounded by a multitude of feet scurrying hither and thither. Through tears, she stared paralyzed at the whirling rainbows of clothes, uniforms, slippers and shoes. Scenting real danger now, she grabbed Riki and Elias firmly by the hand and started to beat a retreat.

"Something terrible's happened!" she gasped. "*Aydi! A casa!* Let's go home! Quick!"

But Riki wanted to stay right where she was, and going against her wishes was never easy. Blanki tugged at her with all her might.

"I don't want to go! *No quieru! No quieru irme!* 'Fraidy cat, that's what you are!" Riki shrieked mockingly. "I like it here! Boom-boom! Like firecrackers! Let go of me, will you! *Deja me!*"

Enraptured by all the uproar and tumult, Riki kept breaking free, so finally Blanki grabbed her by both hands and simply dragged her along, but a moment later she was left empty-handed. She stood stock still for a moment and then called, "Riki! Riki!" Since there was no answer, she set off, amidst all the confusion, racing along the streets in search of her sister. She flitted everywhere. She shouted until she was hoarse. Not a sign of Riki. She had disappeared as if the earth had swallowed her, vanished into thin air!

As tears trickled down her cheeks and Elias wept with exhaustion, Blanki thought how unfair it was that today of all days such a misfortune should befall her. Instead of witnessing untold beauties of the resplendent arrival of the archduke, she had not even seen Franz Ferdinand, and, what was even worse, she had lost her little sister.

Sobbing bitterly, she walked home with a terrible feeling of self-reproach: her parents had entrusted the two younger children to her care, so it was her duty to bring them back safe and sound. Her strong sense of responsibility made this failure weigh even more heavily on her. By the time she reached home, she was completely worn out and terrified.

# Farewell

*Ava Kadishson Schieber*

I had to go to Novi Sad, to deal with family property, including the house that had been put in my name and my sister's. It was early spring 1949, a transitional moment of the postwar era in Yugoslavia. Life was so different from everything that had seemed familiar just ten years earlier.

I went to my hometown to renounce ownership of all of those pieces of Yugoslavia that remained my inheritance and sign it over to the government. My sister's part belonged to her husband. I had already helped him to claim and receive her share as compensation for what he had done to help us during the war.

The legal proceedings regarding our property took years. I had to recover land deeds and establish death certificates for my grandmother, father, and sister. It took countless hours waiting in municipal offices, often with no one willing to move the procedures along. Because I had to travel about sixty miles north from Belgrade to Novi Sad, I only came up during my vacations from work. Between finishing my studies and making a living, there was no other time to do it all. In addition to the pressure on my time, those trips were also a burdensome tax on my meager earnings. Nonetheless, if I wanted something done, I had to go there, always dreading the journey. This trip was to be the last time I would be in the place where I grew up. I felt as though I were visiting a cemetery where no one whom I cared for was buried.

Renouncing everything of value I owned was the price of my freedom. It was the only way I could legally leave a country that had become more and more alien. But giving up everything that represented security was no novelty for me. The war and four years of experiences since had prepared me well for an atmosphere that was veering on the very edge of hostility toward Jews. My alertness to that fact heightened as my understanding of the world matured.

Back in 1944, shortly after the liberation of Belgrade, I had asked for a special permit from the partisan armed forces to travel with a Soviet medical convoy heading north. My goal was to find my father and grandmother, who I hoped were still alive in occupied Hungary. The war was not yet over.

I remember that journey well. I was sitting in an open truck with several Russian soldiers. We were passing battlefields where only recently there must have been military encounters and fierce fighting. Bodies of slain soldiers, dead horses, and demolished armor mingled in a terrible embrace. Still smoldering fires, the eerie sounds of distant guns, and the stench of war were around us. I didn't know on which side the dead belonged. After battles, death unifies uniforms.

The soldiers beside me did not react at all. I had been forewarned that I should delay my journey, but I wanted to see if Father and Grandmother might be alive in Novi Sad, which at this point had reverted back from Hungary to a liberated Yugoslavia.

After a couple of hours driving through the horror and devastation on and off the completely demolished road, we came to a halt. Everyone went to find a place to relieve himself. I didn't dare move away from the truck; I was afraid to be left behind, alone in the field of corpses.

The officer sitting with the driver in the cab approached me. To my surprise, he introduced himself as the doctor of the unit—and started to talk to me in Yiddish. From my documents he had seen the reason for my journey and that I was Jewish as well. He told me that no one in his unit knew that he was a Jew and then asked me not to say anything about my identity to the soldiers with whom I shared the space.

I was shivering from the cold and the sights, not to mention the stench of the past few hours. The doctor gave me his fur coat to wrap myself in. I felt very grateful. No one had been kind to me in many years.

We parted in Novi Sad with a handshake. And now I was left with puzzled thoughts about the Soviet doctor. He had been reluctant to reveal to his comrades in combat that he was a Jew. Something was very wrong.

Upon arriving in Novi Sad on this trip, I was also soon bewildered by my own existence. Maybe this was because of what had happened in this country since its liberation from Nazi occupation. I introduced myself at the headquarters of the local partisan command and asked if there was any evidence of my father's and grandmother's whereabouts. First, of course, I had gone to the house where we had all lived before the war. There, my worst fears became reality.

As the war moved from the Soviet Union, it burst with new force into neighboring countries like Hungary that had collaborated with the Nazi occupiers. Jews who had escaped the earlier roundups were inevitably caught by the Germans and deported. Father and Grandmother were in those last trains to the camps. And then their property was confiscated by the German military. Our house, located in a nice part of town, consisted of two large apartments. I heard what had happened from the tenant who lived on the second floor. When Grandmother and Father were deported to the camps, the Nazis moved in and made an office out of the confiscated apartment. Then, when the partisans came into the city, they took whatever was left in the apartment and ransacked the place.

The tenant was a frightened Hungarian widow. She was allowed to stay in the maid's quarters and had only moved back into her own apartment when the fighting armies were gone. Upon my arrival in Novi Sad, I went to see her, and she invited me to stay with her. Since there was no other place for me to go, I felt deeply grateful for her gesture. Not one person who had been a friend before the war had made such an offer. Even those people who had known me since childhood seemed afraid somehow to invite me. I made the assumption that I probably didn't fit in to anyone's home. It must have been that I looked in much worse shape than I believed myself to be.

I was viewed with suspicion. When I asked, no one knew what had happened to my folks or was willing to give me information. On the other hand, complete strangers were generous in their attitude toward me. One of them was this neighbor, a woman we hardly knew, who not only gave me shelter but had taken responsibility for putting some of my father's suits and valuables into safekeeping. Before the deportation, Grandmother had also left our Persian carpets and fine china with her.

During the war, a changeover in Hungary's administration produced threats even for non-Jewish residents. The German army, which took over from the Hungarian administration, drove many young Hungarians to join the resistance forces. This was the case with the son of the woman who invited me to stay with her. She feared the partisans, even though her son was part of a unit fighting the Nazi soldiers. The war was not over yet.

The tenant also told me that Grandmother's furniture and everything else from the apartment had been taken to a warehouse by the partisan forces. She suggested that I might identify some of the items, and in that way I might be able to get them back and perhaps sell them. As it turned out, I didn't reclaim any of our family's furniture. All I found was what that nice Hungarian woman had taken care of and now offered me.

I left her most of what she had been entrusted with, taking just the photographs and small mementos I could carry. She also gave me information that I took to the partisan general command. Maybe they had more data about my family in their files. I have never forgotten the officer who looked first at my papers, then at me, and said, "Interesting—the Jews are already returning."

Instantly, with rising hope, I asked: "Who is back?"

The man's face flushed and he slowly responded, "You are the first."

I knew then the liberation was not meant for me.

I did not want to move back to Novi Sad. Father and Grandmother were gone. Our family house was now just brick walls.

In the years that followed, a cumulative process of events made my home country intolerable for me. All my hopes of rebuilding a shattered part of my life became more and more unrealistic. There was no one I could go to for any help. I had to take care of my mother because for her, this had been one war too many. She never got over losing her child and husband.

For me the most important point of my future was to finish the studies that had been interrupted by the war. I graduated from the Academy of Art and, after finding a job, succeeded at my work. Not the least of it was that I managed to make a life for myself and my mother. My industry and dedication were appreciated by those in charge, and as my position developed into one of more responsibility and recognition, I was asked to join the Communist Party. While this was considered an honor, in this evolving political moment the invitation was also a minefield. I was very careful in the way I expressed my appreciation for the nomination, claiming not to be ready for the honor. This strategy bought me some time, but I knew I was being watched from then on. I was not forgiven for turning down the nomination.

Then, slowly, I found myself isolated at my office, given a room alone and no real project to work on. It was obvious that I didn't belong. I knew I never would. There was no one to be with or share opinions with, no one to confide in about how to structure my life or even to exchange views of artistic concepts and expressions. In the postwar Communist domain, the art field was archaic. I kept that opinion to myself.

I had my dreams but kept those a secret as well. I couldn't even trust the person I was in love with; he had no clue about where my mind was. When I visited his home, some of his relatives would call out to him: "Your Jew is here." They didn't mean to be derogatory; they were just very simple people. When I went to say good-bye to his parents just before my mother and I left for Israel, his mother cried and asked me to reconsider the move. His father couldn't understand why I was leaving a good position at work in order to go to a desert country, and one, moreover, that was at war with all its surrounding neighbors.

My lover didn't believe I was going to leave him and the country. He didn't really know me. I was in love, but we were never honestly intimate as human beings. I could never trust him. This was my state of mind during my last trip to Novi Sad. I was there with one single purpose: to sign legal papers. There was no one to say goodbye to.

After a day of traipsing up and down so many staircases in municipal buildings and after signing a multitude of documents, I was drained. At that moment, what I looked forward to was the luxury of staying overnight in a hotel instead of traveling back to Belgrade in the dark. Ordinarily, I would have had my dinner in the room, eating out of a paper bag in my improvised way. But at the end of that day I gave myself the additional luxury of a meal in the hotel restaurant. I wanted to sit at a table, as though that would endow me with some dignity. While in the dining room, indulging myself in an unfamiliar way, I noticed someone standing across from my table; it was a man I knew only as Little Brother. I remembered that the nickname had seemed funny to me when we were first introduced at work in Belgrade a year or two ago. He was very tall and serene and his image didn't fit his being addressed as "Buddy." And yet everybody called him that. He asked if he could join me—it would be nice to have dinner together. I was surprised when he approached me; it was the first time we had ever talked to each other. In fact, we had not even seen each other for a couple of months.

At work, if we met in the corridors we would only occasionally have exchanged hellos. We both worked at a large government enterprise. He was in the weekly news department, mostly writing. My work consisted of building architectural models or details of theatrical sets that would substitute for the larger ones in the film studios. With these different assignments, Buddy and I didn't really have any contact at work or anyplace else.

Before he was transferred to Novi Sad he had heard that I had resigned from my job. We both knew that being transferred to a small town was a kind of exile—a demotion for him. He didn't mind, he said; in fact, he welcomed the isolation. It would give him more opportunity to write. He wanted to know why I had left. I completely lacked the skill of small talk, but after almost eight years of my own silent existence, I had developed a keen ear. Just as musicians can detect a false ringing sound, I could distinguish lies from truth. Little Brother did not try to get information from me. Everything he said and did told me he was sincere. Here was someone who was an isolated island—just like me. The difference was that I had made a decision to abandon isolation—I wanted to move away from being disconnected. And so I was leaving for Israel, where no one was going to call me Jew. As long as I had the chance, I would no longer stay in a place that didn't want me.

Making this break meant that I had given away any and all symbols of security. I'd abandoned a career in my profession. I'd let go of the man I had fallen in love with two years before and was still emotionally involved with; and just a couple of hours ago, I'd signed away all the real estate I owned, relinquishing it to the government I opposed.

Strangely, I felt happy to have thrown all of these things away. They had become burdens; they were hindering my freedom. I couldn't stay in a place that was trying to change the core of my being. Years of starvation, hard work, and fear had left me with a determination not to yield to any force that was out to break my mind.

Despite the enormously destructive effort of the Nazi doctrine to strip me of my dignity and free thinking, they were left almost unimpaired. I wasn't going to let the Communists destroy my will either.

Maybe it was my ignorance that led me not to consider life's oppressive forces. I had discarded everything I had. It never entered my mind that I had thrown away everything in exchange for taking a serious risk. I was going to an unknown place and building a new life, with no one to ask for advice about what and how to do it. When the war started, I had made a bold move, but now my life was not really endangered. In peril was my choice of how to live.

There was a long silence when I told Buddy about my leaving for Israel. His reaction surprised me. He reached across the table and took both my hands in his. The way he looked at me that first moment startled me—making me think he was going to kiss my hands in the middle of the restaurant. In postwar Yugoslavia something like that would have been unthinkable. As if reading my mind, he smiled, and then became sad. He held my hands a long time and said: "We're both outcasts, only you have a place to go to. I do not."

As the evening advanced he talked with more ease. He originally came from rural Serbia, and had been with the partisans throughout the entire war. I tried to imagine the soft-spoken Buddy as a fighter all during those very difficult years. It was one of the faces he kept hidden. Of all those who had joined at the beginning of that extensive struggle, there were so few survivors. If not the enemy, then the epidemics took countless lives.

Buddy's whole attitude was so different from that of the few other war veterans I knew. I was bewildered by his statement that he was an outcast like me. Why wouldn't he be accepted? After all, he had fought for the political power now ruling the country.

It was getting late and the dining room was almost empty when Buddy quietly told me why he didn't fit into Yugoslav society and had no place to go. He was homosexual. This time it was I who reached across the table and held his hands. It had taken a great deal of trust for him to reveal that. Even the slightest suspicion was dangerous. Homosexuality was not talked about, and if rumors started, people were jailed or just disappeared. Before the war the attitude was unforgiving; after the war homosexuality became totally unacceptable. I felt honored by his trust, and it occurred to me that I was being more intimate with this man I was talking to for the first time in my life than I ever was with my lover of two years.

The dining room emptied, and it was time for us to get up and leave. Buddy walked me to my room and I was not surprised when he asked me if he could just stay with me for the rest of the night. I knew that if he spent the night in my room it could help him silence any possible rumors. That he had dined with and stayed overnight with a woman would have been noticed and probably registered. Our connection could silence suspicion and give him some time.

I didn't mind. We shared loneliness and his life-threatening secret. It was part of a relationship that existed only for a couple of hours but with trust for a lifetime.

It must have been early morning when he left the room. I didn't wake up. It was still dark when the alarm rang and I had to hurry to catch my bus. I had paid for my room the day before, but there was no time for coffee. I was glad that Buddy had left; there was nothing more for us to say to each other. It was only respect for the trust and understanding of isolation and alienation, of not belonging, that had created the closeness between us.

He was going to be my one cherished memory of Novi Sad: falling asleep and being hugged by someone who was as isolated from society as I was, a human being with an overwhelming need to share an extremely dangerous secret. It felt good to have had the opportunity to reciprocate his trust.

The bus station was close by and I took a seat. Then, as I lowered the window, I saw Buddy hurrying toward the bus. He handed me some rolled-up newspapers. Unshaven, he looked drawn and old. I was moved that he had brought the papers—it was so thoughtful of him to provide me with reading material for the ride. When I saw the flowers—still bright with morning dew in the damp paper—I was overwhelmed. The way they looked and were wrapped, I knew that Buddy must have taken them from somebody's garden.

We were both smiling—as we must have both forgotten how to cry—when he kissed my hand.

# Remembering Silivri at the Hotel Majestic

*Ruth Behar*

Growing up in New York in a Cuban-Jewish family, I knew I was a child of many exiles. On my mother's side, the family was Ashkenazi, from eastern Europe. Baba, my grandmother, was from Poland, and Zayde, my grandfather, from Russia. They each arrived alone in Cuba in the 1920s, hoping to bring their families to safety on the island as conditions worsened in Europe. They spoke Yiddish and the language meant so much to them that Zayde courted Baba by giving her copies of the Yiddish newspaper, *The Forward,* that he special-ordered from New York. Never having met Jews from other diasporas, they believed all Jews spoke Yiddish, that it was a condition of being Jewish. They were shocked when my mother decided to marry my father, a Sephardic Jew. His parents were from Turkey, and claimed Spanish ancestry as well as a Jewish identity. They didn't speak Yiddish. How was that possible?

Abuela and Abuelo, my Sephardic grandparents, spoke Ladino. This was a version of Spanish preserved by ancestors who'd been expelled from Spain in 1492, just before Columbus set out on his first voyage to the Americas. Sefarad means Spain in Hebrew and Sephardic Jews are the Jews who chose exile from Spain. They could have stayed if they'd converted to Catholicism, but they refused, seeking a new home elsewhere. Yet the Sephardim were so nostalgic for their homeland that they held on to Spanish, the language of those who expelled them. That is why Ladino is also known as Judeo-Spanish, meaning that for Sephardic Jews, Spanish became a Jewish language.

My identity is a mix of these two Jewish cultures—the Ashkenazi and the Sephardic, the first forged in the world of Christian Europe, the second in the world of the Muslim Ottoman Empire. That mix of cultures is, in turn, mixed with Cuban culture. All four grandparents chanced to migrate to Cuba in the 1920s. They couldn't enter the United States because of the harsh quotas that limited the numbers of immigrants from eastern and southern Europe, but Cuba was prosperous then, basking in sugar wealth and launching a profitable tourist industry where rum and Coke flowed during Prohibition. The long struggle for national independence led to religious pluralism. Once Catholicism ceased to be the sole religion, the door opened to Jewish immigration. My grandparents, along with thousands of other Jewish migrants, found their way to the island.

Abuela, my paternal grandmother, was from Silivri, a small town near Istanbul. Her parents had arranged for her to sail to Havana and wed a Sephardic Jew living there, but he grew impatient for her to arrive and married someone else. An uncle in Havana took her in. To pass the time, she sang sad Sephardic love songs and accompanied herself on the oud she'd brought from Turkey. One of these songs, with its haunting verses about a young woman who disobeyed her father and ended up jailed in a tower in the sea, might have attracted the moody man who was to become my Abuelo, my paternal grandfather, also from Silivri, who proposed marriage after passing by and hearing her sing this song of heartbreak. They married and went to live in a tenement in Old Havana that looked out at the sea. They had four children, the third child my father. Abuela stopped played the oud after becoming a wife and mother. My father says she was too busy and that her oud hung from a nail on the wall in their apartment on Calle Oficios. She never sang again. Never saw her parents again. Her story haunted me for years. I have just completed a novel, *Across So Many Seas*, inspired by all the silences of her story and the oud she once played.

Many years later, in the late 1980s, in the last years of his life, Abuelo chose to live in the Hotel Majestic on Ocean Drive, in the section of Miami known as South Beach. It wasn't the South Beach of today. The art deco hotels facing the sapphire sea had not yet been declared historical patrimony. They were dilapidated and moldy and smelled of regret, as happens to everything by the sea that is allowed to go to waste. Abuelo didn't seem to notice. After retiring from his job as a factory worker at Goodman's Matzo, he told Abuela he wanted to leave Canarsie and go south to sunny Miami. They'd vacationed there and hadn't it been beautiful? But Abuela wanted to stay in Brooklyn. Her beloved younger daughter, my Aunt Fanny, lived next door with her husband and children. Abuela didn't want to be far from them. "*Vaz a Miami cuando yo me muera,*" she told Abuelo. "You'll go to Miami when I die."

And so it happened. Abuela died of cancer in 1981 and Abuelo packed his bags. His room at the Hotel Majestic was just big enough to fit a bed, a TV, a nightstand, and a dorm-sized refrigerator. He said he didn't need more. He ate his meals down the block at Puerto Sagua, a Cuban restaurant whose owners once had a restaurant with the same name in Havana.

Abuelo was an elegant man, lean, with a full head of hair and sparkling dark eyes. He was jovial and quick to laugh. He wore a clean *guayabera* dress shirt every day. I found him charming, but my father couldn't stand to be around him. He had been forced to go peddle blankets door-to-door with Abuelo in Havana when he was a young man. He had wanted to study architecture and never forgave his father for denying him his education. My father never called his father Papá or Papi but by his name, Isaac.

Toward the end, Abuelo became senile. He was aware of his fading memory. To keep a grip on reality, each morning he bought *El Nuevo Herald*, the Spanish version of the *Miami Herald*. He clutched it in his hands to know what month, day, and year it was. He spent his days sitting on the front porch of the hotel, staring at the sea. "*Me recuerda Silivri,*" he'd say, his gaze foggy. Siliviri ... where both he and Abuela were from. From the coast of Miami, he saw the sea of his youth, and remembered the boats docked in Silivri and the fishermen casting their nets.

Whenever I'd visit Abuelo at the Hotel Majestic, inevitably a time came to say goodbye, and I'd say to him, "*Hasta mañana,*" and he'd always reply, "*Si Dios quiere*"—if God wills it.

There was no certainty in life. You might not be around tomorrow. That decision wasn't in mortal hands. It was in God's hands.

I was convinced that a Sephardic sensibility informed Abuelo's melancholy approach to departures, as if each and every goodbye was the last. I think I perceived this because I had a counterpoint with my other grandparents, Baba and Zeide, my Ashkenazi grandparents from Poland and Russia who were Yiddish speakers. They didn't offer emotionally-charged farewells. They gave you a kiss and said bye.

Being the daughter of a Sephardic father and an Ashkenazi mother, I grew up trying to figure out what cultural characteristics belonged to each group, never sure if these differences were a matter of personality, or if they had a social basis. Was my father's angry spirit and unforgiving nature a result of his being Sephardic? My Ashkenazi family thought so. They viewed themselves as even-tempered people who didn't hold grudges and forgave easily.

In the absence of a deep familiarity with the Sephardim, I realized I'd inherited not a cultural legacy so much as what scholars call Sephardism, a Jewish version of Orientalism, a set of distorted images and mirages of the people and places that are part of my genealogy. My Sephardic heritage still remains mysterious to me.

As I think back now, so many years later, to Abuelo spending his last days at the Hotel Majestic, I feel such sorrow for him, looking out to the sea day after day, so alone, his mind slowly unraveling, losing all sense of time, but always remembering the lost home of Silivri. My father, with his anger, never reconciled with his father, though he did cry desperately the day of the funeral. How I wish these men of my patrilineal line had passed on more to me of what they knew of the Sephardic heritage. Instead, it is through ethnography and history and creative writing that I have claimed my cultural heritage and Sephardic ancestry from Spain and that I have sought to innovate on a religious background that didn't offer me much space for self-expression as a woman. I will continue on my journey, moving beyond the silences of the fathers, to find the words to speak of a community that has made the remembrance of loss the core of its spiritual quest.

# In Search of Marie J[1]

*Michèle Sarde*

Jenny says: as a child, we used to call you Michou. But we also named you Marie and then Reine as a third name, because of my grandmother, Reyna. In proper French, that gives Marie-Reine.

Michou is still a child who loves dressing up in old clothes, when she discovers a long mane of blonde hair in the attic of our house in Brie.

—What's this, mama, this shock of hair?

"Oh, nothing! It belonged to your grandmother Marie. The other one."

Abandoned to moths, the beautiful tresses have disappeared since then. They will not be found in the suitcase where my mother Jenny consigned her memories during the crossing of silence in which she confined both of us.

As we broke this fast of memory together, I was able to tell the story that she herself had handed down to me in a hundred-page manuscript added to a long testimonial that I obtained from her, then recorded and transcribed. To this bundle of memories were added the contents of a suitcase, or rather, a coffer, half filled with photographs, letters, various documents, dormant under the dust of half a century. A true Ali Baba treasure chest.

Little by little as she recounted, we took out of the suitcase all the archival documents that brought light to her own story and that of her people who came from the former Jewish city of Salonica, the Hellenic town of the Roman Empire, known today as Thessaloniki.

In the end all that was left were the albums and documents belonging to "the other family," "the Bulgarian one," the family of Jacques, her husband, "the love of her life." Another family. Another story. The one of my father, and his people, the one of Marie and Moise, my paternal grandparents.

---

1   Translated from the French by Domnica Radulescu.

From Jacques' story, which dated from before her time, Jenny only retained some bits and pieces. She lacked the leading thread, the foundation of the story. But she possessed plenty of anecdotes, tiny memories, which together, would allow the recreation of the whole, once the basis had been established.

Jenny knew that her mother-in-law, Marie, was from Romania, that her father-in-law, Moise, was from Bulgaria, that they also spoke Judeo-Spanish, the ancient Castilian dialect from the fifteenth century, carried in exile following the expulsion of the Jews by the Catholic kings in 1492.

This language, improperly called "Ladino," a term which only refers to the liturgical language, the Judeo-Spanish people called it *Judesmo*. The Bulgarians called it *espanyoliko nuestro*, and it is how I will refer to it from now on.

Jenny knew that for a certain reason, Marie and Moise had left Bulgaria for France during the twenties, surprisingly detaining Italian citizenship, thus allowing her to meet and marry Jacques, their only son.

Jenny knew that in the middle of the German occupation, they had taken a repatriation train to Italy, as was the case for Italian Jewish nationals.

And then she knew that they had disappeared without a trace.

Certain details about her mother-in-law and father-in-law had been kept, here and there, in the snare of her storytelling, details which I only identified upon a second reading, when its existence was recorded, and the other story started to insert itself in the memory of this new text. These bursts of memory will be faithfully included in the story.

I knew nothing more about Marie than a bottomless absence, the young blonde woman whose long mesh of orphan hair I had once touched as a child. Neither did I know anything about her life- and death-partner, Moise. However, they did know me since I was born before they were thrown into the abyss. It is why I cannot really say, like Ivan Jablonka, that they are strictly "the grandparents that I never had."

*The Scents of Memories*

But I have everything to learn about them. I hardly know where they come from, I know very little about how they lived, not at all how they died and even less whether they may have descendants spread in the four corners of the world.

As a little girl, after the war, I desperately waited for my Nonamali, or in adult language, Grandmother Marie, and for my grandfather Moise. I was barely three years old the last time I saw them, or rather that they saw me. At the end of the apocalypse, I was six. I kept waiting until the age of eleven, until my mother Jenny threw in my face the reason why they were never going to return.

Occasionally, as Jenny told her story, in an answer to one of my questions, an enlightening bit of information would emerge, which came back from time to time:

"You are asking me how was Marie? I told you time and again. She was like you ... You are her spitting image. And not just physically!"

As for Jacques, their son, and my father, one should not bring up the subject of his parents, nor ask him any questions. He was "fragile," Jenny would say in a blank voice.

I obeyed this interdiction. I did not ask him anything about his parents' story, nor about his own life before my own appearance in his, and before our biographies became entangled.

—It's enough for him that you are there, Jenny kept saying. You resemble his mother Marie, so much. It does him a world of good.

For a long time, I thought that my presence made up for her absence, that I was filling a void of some sort. Jacques died prematurely of a massive stroke. And I am convinced that he died of grief. When he disappeared, I had nothing left, I was myself in the void, a double, a triple void.

And then Jenny, my inexhaustible source, died in her turn, of a peaceful death, in her own bed, and then I decided to start an official search of his disappeared parents of whom I only possessed these shreds of memory.

On December nineteenth 2005 I received an e-mail in English from a certain Deborah F. who was informing me that the Italian center of research had provided the following information about the deportation of my grandparents.

> Moise Benrey was born in Bulgaria in an unknown town. He was arrested at Argegno near Como on the 4th of September by the Nazis. He was detained in the prison of San Vittore in Milan, then in a transit camp at Bolzano from where he was deported to Auschwitz on the 24th of October 1944. The same thing happened to his wife.

The chief archivist says she does not believe that there was a concentration camp at Argegno but rather in the border zone between Switzerland and Italy. Her information derives from M. Edmond Tagger, who gave testimony in 1974. She asked if you could provide her with the place of birth of M. and Mme Benrey.

"The same thing happened to his wife." Never had I felt the extent to which Marie, myself, us women, we are negligible quantity in the death register as in the register of life, as I did in that draft of a testimonial.

I receive this dry message like a prayer from beyond the grave, a new exhortation to return from silence, to investigate, explore, inquire, research, imagine, advance in a different direction. A new challenge. It calls me back to my duty to mourn and to bury, then to discover the living beneath the shroud that I need to create from all the shreds. Memory surveyor, Antigone, relayed by Atalanta, goes in search of Eurydice. I take her to task, or rather I leave with her on journeys to the countries where these shadows were once alive.

I have never found a trace of the flamboyant mane of hair, but I have discovered, in Ali Baba's chest, the face of its owner with her golden necklace, framed by the tresses that fell to her waist and that I had once had the joy of holding in my hands.

With these last rites I cast off the anchorages for the great adventure: find my two disappeared relatives across the multifaceted Europe of the previous century in the last millennium of human history. And I embarked on a search for this golden fleece towards the country of Colchis, on the shore of this sea called Black, not very far away from the rock against which Medea crushed her ship, in the exact place where Marie received her first kiss from a Romanian officer of the Admiralty.

But I did not leave alone on this new *Argo*. I will reveal my traveling companions little by little during the crossing. Like the "Righteous among people" of my hidden childhood. At every stage of the journey, like sea birds, they welcomed or escorted the virtual ship whose prow figure was a magnificent mane, the flamboyant tresses of a young woman of twenty, who later became a shadow in a landscape of ashes.

Thus, like modern alchemists, we sailed on our ship in search of gold, the gold of a mesh of hair, the gold of a necklace, the gold of a wedding band left intact in the embers.

We traveled in search of Marie and Moise, of their childhood, of their hopes, of their loves. In search of their joys and sorrows in the past world that they inhabited. In search of their future, of their survivors, of certain genes that they scattered on this planet and that allowed them to persist.

I call the Antigone syndrome the force that drives and pushes me today to pursue Marie and Moise, to enable them to resurrect, and to build their grave. A work of memory in the shape of mourning and resiliency. But mostly a work of bringing into the world the Lost Ones.

# Sarajevo Underground[1]

*Andrea Jeftanovic*

> "It is in your interest to continue on a different journey
> —he said, after seeing me cry—
> if you want to flee from this savage place:
> because this beast, for which you clamor,
> doesn't allow another to pass along his path."
> Dante Alighieri

Welcome to Hell! Written in red letters, it was the slogan that I found upon my arrival to Sarajevo.

## First Circle

"Ready?" Edis indicated to me to look down in order to not trip upon the first beam. I grasp the steel frame and descend, letting go of his wrinkled hand. He suggests that we continue along the meters of the tunnel that are still passable. We prepare a bag with

---

1 Translated from the Spanish by Jacqueline Nanfito.

water and dried fruit; we walk among the nettles in the yard until we reach the entrance. I think that he says without saying "I will serve as your guide along the places where we will be able to pass." Then he continues: "Only one person at a time can enter." My shoes sink into the mud, I hear the sound of a highway, it's difficult to maintain my balance on the muddy ground.

Edis tells me that the engineer, Nedžad Branković, sketched the tunnel and organized its construction with the idea of paving the way to the aggressor's front and successfully laying siege to the city.

The snipers never stopped shooting, as they knew that a tunnel was being built but had no idea as to how it was happening. While they thought that the tunnel was taking form in a certain direction, in reality, it went in another. At that point, around three hundred people died. Branković managed to cross twenty-four times in a day by way of the exterior line that divided the two sides. On July 20, 1993, at nine in the evening, after seven months of arduous work, two excavators that advanced from opposite sides met and shook hands. Sarajevo had a window onto the free world.

I descended the hills towards Sarajevo. I circled down the curves of the geography of Mount Igman, which, during the Balkan War, between 1992 and 1995, was surrounded by tanks and snipers. When we were amid the Dinaric Alps, I caught a glimpse of the urban outline with asphalt bands, blocks of perforated bricks and wavy metallic sheets. From west to east the Miljacka River drew a crystalline line that divided the city in two. I descended among the steep, rocky gorges, and at every curve in the path there was a contingent of soldiers aboard NATO tanks. We advanced along the reddish stretch of land once occupied by peasants and shepherds. Curved, steep, vertiginous, Sarajevo resembled the geography of Santiago: a city with the form of a basin, cordoned-off by mountains and a river that divides it in two.

I traveled in a dilapidated bus that wound its way from Split, on the Adriatic Coast; I passed by towns destroyed in the last war. At the border, a couple of toothless soldiers laughed at my passport; I searched in them for some tribal recognition and only felt a distant rejection. We advanced at an unhurried pace along phantasmal highways in which the grass was beginning to grow among the concrete roadways. At the first stop I contemplated a landscape composed of a "still life": the Mostar bridge, known for its elegance since the Turkish Ottoman Empire, was uneven and patched with rubber tires.

I came in search of the tunnel. Because, almost like an image taken from the film, *Underground*, by Emir Kusturica, the city of Sarajevo resisted the attack during years of war, in part, due to the tunnel. An underground tunnel eight hundred meters long, one meter wide and a meter-and-a-half tall, which extended from the airport in Dobrinja, until the free zone of Butmir.

On the surface, hell; under the earth, a piece of heaven.

*Welcome to Hell?*, I wanted to ask when I approached an office of tourism and was greeted by a salutation of mangled words. The graffiti continued to palpitate in my pupils. They extended a tourist map with indications for me to find the room: "Advance two blocks and turn to the left towards a stone building with a rusty door, number 76." I climbed up a shadowy staircase and an older woman opened the door. Her head was covered in a silk scarf with a red bird perched on an olive-green branch. I smelled the scent of turmeric concentrated in the apartment. She indicated the floor with a slight arch of her eye. I understood that I needed to take off my shoes and don a pair of colorful slippers in order to walk along the mosaic tile flooring. I set down my suitcase in the assigned room and went out to the avenue.

"*O Tunnel da Rat?*", I asked the first available taxi driver. I repeated "o tunnel da Rat" in Dobrinja. My reference disconcerted the driver. So, I added some gestures to my phrase. At some point he understood me because he took me to the outskirts of the city, where I had heard that it was located. During the journey I observed the buildings that arose like enormous expired animals. The tower of the newspaper, *Oslobodjenje*, resembled a dinosaur collapsed upon the ground. They say that after the bombardment, journalists continued working in the basement. The driver also pointed out the

National Library, devoured by the fire. I imagined the volumes crackling amidst the flames.

We continued on our way, passing by the façade of the Gavrilo Princip Museum, the building perforated by the military assault. I got out to take a photo of the emblematic corner and walked in the footprints of the Princip on the cement, the place where the member of the young Bosnia shot the Archduke Francisco Fernando and his wife on June 28, 1914. Two parallel traces in the walkway. I separated my feet from the path and returned to the car.

I left behind the corner of the ultimatum at Sarajevo.

After bordering a suburban zone—I noticed it because of the low density of the constructions—the driver stopped the car and told me that I could not leave that perimeter. I got out somewhat disappointed and inquired about the tunnel to the first pedestrians that were walking along the dusty pavement. I didn't make myself clear, and I spoke more carefully: "*O tunnel da Rat.*" There was a small uproar amid the individuals that asked one another about the whereabouts of that place. After nearly an hour, a young taxi driver offered to take me. I got into his dilapidated gray Mercedes Benz and we traveled along a dirt road with brick houses sprinkled sparsely throughout the area. After several intersections he stopped in front of a small, two-story house.

It's here? *Da, da, ovdje.* (Yes, yes, here.) Edis Kolar had caught wind of a rumor that a female foreigner was searching for him, and he came out to greet me. He was young, medium height, with a warm smile. He guided me along the passageways of the house in which they had improvised a modest museum with photographs and objects. I followed the wall, observing a camouflaged jacket, a bronze teapot, and two grenades. He showed me a construction plan, stopped for a recollection of the Chilean carabiners, and I remained silent because that symbol provoked mixed emotions in me.

Edis asked me to write down my name on paper because he couldn't understand my pronunciation. I jotted down the sixteen letters of my last name, and he put his finger above the final "c," wanting to confirm my writing. Indeed, the accent mark over that "c" was missing, a habit that I began losing with writing at the computer. It must signify something to lose that accent.

He is very young. How old must he have been around the time of the conflict? I'm calculating his age when he presents me to the rest of his family, his grandparents, Alija and Šida, and his parents, Emina and Edin. During times of war, they would await the emergence of travelers from the tunnel with a teapot over an open fire and a piece of bread.

In the city, hell; underneath a patio, heaven.

## Second Circle

One must follow the course of subterranean waters, the laws of the abyss. We bordered the second leveled area. There is an opening and railroad cars appear. The stalled trains go nowhere and together they seem like an apocalyptic postcard of an abandoned station following a disaster. Edis adjusts the screws and moves the debris from the platform, we climb into a car that glides along rusty rails. The car continues along until it becomes entrapped in a narrow pass, and we pull some cables to ascend among the skylights. The shaky light of the lantern guides us among the paths. An underground moan unsettles us, the doors in the passageways are open traps. The beam that runs above the unexpected rooms of hell. We advance with inadequate and confusing maps, where the heavens sink, and the abysms emerge. The frost on the walls appears like darts of fire above the timeworn coins on the ground. Losing one's head at every curve, and with each step, the earth sliding beneath our feet. Landscapes dissolved by the drops of water from the stalactites. The palms of the hands of pious hostages.

He tells me about a couple that married in the free territory after traveling in the car along the railways at breakneck speed. They were wed in the middle of the tunnel, neutral territory. I see a photo of the bride, with her white dress and a bouquet of yellow flowers, seated on the lap of her betrothed with her arm around his shoulder. They both smile from the chair made of woven nuts and bolts. The

tunnel also facilitated the trip of government officials and members of parliament out of the country for important negotiations with NATO and world leaders. Edis stops over the rails and continues his story: "You see, circulation was in one direction at the time, in groups of twenty to one hundred persons, and it took them two hours to cross from one side to another, transporting twenty tons."

Each one of the pedestrians had to push between two hundred and three hundred kilos of cargo, traveling along a path of curves, descents, and ascents. I listen to how amidst a dust cloud twice the tunnel was flooded and closed for a couple of days, until the extraction pumps cleared it. He tells me that necessary maintenance halted its use between eight and eleven in the morning. He shows me some copper tubing that was part of a donation of cable by the German government, which permitted the construction of an electrical system and telephone lines.

He pauses and drinks water from the canteen as if recalling a forgotten fatigue. I am grateful for the silence while I observe the tubing. He stops at a wall and signals me forward. I follow his hand, which points to a dark place.

"The night was the best time for moving people and heavy cargo, because the movements were less visible for the enemy, given that they knew of the existence of this corridor. One winter morning, a grenade killed a group of individuals that waited at the entrance; we no longer permitted long lines during the light of day." Edis sinks in the depths of his patio while the dust of memory hovers above the streets of Sarajevo, covering the minarets, the dead of the market buried under a mound of tomatoes. The abuses had an impact, opening holes in the fog, amidst the chilly breeze. In 1994 twenty-two persons had been in line at a bakery, when a grenade exploded, and all that remained was a heap of scattered breadcrumbs.

On distinct occasions I pass by the corner imagining those atoms of life.

"Anyone could shoot in a city under siege; on the rooftops there was always someone counting my vertebrae and aiming at my silhouette."

He tells me that he used to cross the pathway of the snipers at two hundred kilometers an hour, stretched out on the backseat, sweating profusely, touching the bulletproof vest and observing the tram cars heaped together. Sarajevo was the death trap of the Balkans, the city with its entrails exposed. The Federal Republic of Yugoslavia was fractured into six pieces of a puzzle that never fit together due to a lack of factories.

"Let the crusades of the great Serbia stop, as there is no wood with which to make caskets."

I have been visiting Sarajevo for years, when the men in the family toasted with šljivovica following the meal and vowed "next year in Yugoslavia". Sarajevo was a promised land, the destination by which we swore at every gathering with that crystal clear Serbian liqueur, made from moonshine and prunes. The toast motivated the clinking of glasses before the alcohol went to the head of the adults, brimming with vivid remembrances of a childhood around the Drina and the Miljacka, rivers which became blurred with the Mapocho River and became navigable. Or rather, the stroll down Maršala Tita Avenue, which merged with Bernardo O'Higgins Boulevard, wide pathways in which there was traffic both ways. Saint Sava, the familiar patron of Serbia, appears descending from the Andes Mountains and stands in the middle of the monument to the war of Chacabuco.

Sarajevo became present each time I accompanied my father to the Russian Orthodox Church at the intersection of Holanda and Doctor Johow streets in Ñuñoa, a neighborhood in Santiago. The small temple with its needlelike cross, a dome of two spheres and a pope with a long beard who dispersed incense, until everything became immersed in an aromatic cloud while he repeated prayers in ancient Russian. For Holy Week we would eat hand-painted eggs, while the people greeted one another with: "*Hristos Vaskrse!*" ("Christ has risen!") and "*Vaistinu vaskrse!*" ("He has risen!")

To believe in two religions is like having two heads.

## Third Circle

We have passed by a grotto of sharp rocks. The temperature drops here. An icy breeze passes through the catacombs.

In 1984 one watched the winter Olympics in Sarajevo on a Zenit television with lifeless colors. The images of the future war will occur in the same snow-covered mountains that I remember during the fourteenth edition of the Winter Games, with their little flags and the image of the mascot, a small wolf named Vučko. Could Vučko guess what was to come? The mascot, designed by the Slovenian illustrator, Jože Trobec, was perhaps the announcement of danger lying in wait; Vučko, the fierce wolf, the wolf that would howl when the moon appeared over the valley of Sarajevo.

We were able to follow the journey of the Olympic athletes on the television screen at home: from the highest point of Igman Mountain to the mountainside where snipers would shoot years later. The skiers would line up to descend the slope of Trebevićč. In that opportunity Yugoslavia won a silver medal in the men's giant slalom event, thanks to the athlete, Jure Franko.

I tell Edis that my paternal side of the family would make jokes about the Balkan formula: six republics, five nations, four languages, three religions, two alphabets and one party. They would say: "It's an encumbrance to be the city that triggered the First World War." They would ask one another obsessively: "Do you have Ustaša or Četnik relatives?" Sunday they would stretch out in lawn chairs after a lunch of sauteed peppers and sip šljivovica celebrating while they chant *dobro, dobro.* (Good, Good.) Midafternoon they would mount horses bareback, dig in their spurs and kick the sides of the animals yanking the reins from one side to another. Their heads were covered with a red felt cap, their beard emerging, their gaze clouded from an excess of alcohol. They galloped about, striking the horse with the riding crop, speaking in that language filled with sonorous "z"s:

*Ja sam. Ja sam. Sam ja? Za, zabada, zabada.* (I am I. I am? Always, free, always, party.)

Saint Nicholas, with his purple cloak and beckoning black eyes. Saint Sava, patron saint of Serbia and founder of a monastery, who abandoned the court to don a religious habit, appeared descending near a lagoon to preach compassion and the truth at the monument of the battle of Chacabuco. The ascension of Christ, like a pagan god that invites us to a celebration each new year, the Messiah that arrived not via Jerusalem, rather by way of the Andes mountains.

When I could finally travel to Yugoslavia, Yugoslavia no longer existed. I arrived at Sarajevo looking to visit familiar sites: an apartment on the third floor of a busy street, an artisanal brick factory, a hotel in the ancient quarter of the city, properties confiscated by the Tito regime. More than a patrimonial vindication, I was impelled by an emotional itinerary.

First of all, I went in search of the small brick factory in the outskirts of the city. As a point of reference, a black-and-white photo of some ovens with clay among meadows. The taxi circled several hills following a map of the city folded into four sections. When

*The Scents of Memories*

we arrived at the address we came upon a cemetery. The driver looked down. The green hill was covered with numerous graves with Orthodox crosses, Muslim half-moons and stars of David. We walked among the tombstones, which were already covered with moss and marks made by humidity. Only a few centimeters separated one from the other. The inscriptions with the dates 1992, 1994, 1995 were repeated as though they were epitaphs of death. We walked among the tombstones without completing the perimeter of death that ended in a distant point in the valley. We retreated in silence.

The apartment above Maršal Tito Avenue was part of a building that still had perforations produced by the mortars, an image that we had seen in the reports of war on CNN. When I arrived, I rang the bell of the intercom system. In the face of the impossibility of understanding due to the traffic and language, I managed to climb the three floors so that they would open the immense door. The current residents weren't thrilled about allowing me to enter. I stood there, at a thirty-degree angle that permitted me to see a wooden floor, high ceilings, and a mobile with red letters with the phrase *I love Paris*.

The Hotel, named Europa, was situated near Baščaršija, the great market that is a mixture of the Turkish Ottoman tradition, which is the heart of the ancient quarters of the city. During the war the hotel housed two thousand Muslims, when its capacity was that of two hundred persons. It is said that almost one hundred and twenty grenades fell upon the building. I walked among the rooms and hallways, and it was still possible to find scraps of children's clothing, blankets, slippers missing their mates, piles of mattresses, beverage cans, kitchen utensils. The roof was covered with weeds. In a bathroom of blue artifacts, I found a dove plastered against the bathtub. Perhaps one would have to learn to decipher the anthropology of waste in order to read the message of debris.

Yugoslavia kaput.

## Fourth Circle

If you succeed in advancing, you will find one door after another, until you arrive at the door of your choosing.

Rats gnaw at the threshold of the other edge. A pair of phosphorescent tracks illuminate my pants on the two sides of the basement. We make our way among a foggy frieze. I see a broad moat that winds like an arch and embraces the meadow. According to my guide, the water descends from one circle to another.

There were few letters from Nenda. He was my father's twin and lived in Croatia at the time of war. His letters had exquisite handwriting, they evaded the hill by means of United Nations' convoys and arrived at my home on Santa Brígida Street in Santiago, Chile. At times he would write to me from a clinic, other times from an island. He would tell me that there was a hole opened by a mortar shell that passed between two hospital beds. Slowly we advance and Edis indicates to me the firebreak lines. "In order to leave this circle, we have to cross through flames." I remain in the curved frame of the doors connecting hinges and murmurs.

I recall an unmarried uncle that never drank šljivovica and looked at the bottle with distrust, and one day he whispered a phrase that I have archived: "The Ustashas in the Second World War, used to carry out the killings after having imbibed that alcohol. Men that never killed a fly until they drank. Do you know what it is to see an official photo of young soldiers posing with a smile in front of a mound of skulls? To go out into the city and come across the heads of your neighbors nailed upon gnarled stakes?"

Josip Broz Tito, burly body, face of burnished steel, with the air of high society. Always dressed impeccably in white. Dark glasses perched upon his nose. A wide belt circling his military uniform. Hands that shook when he gave his speeches. Gold rings that also shook, his military Maršal insignias on his jacket. Tito repeating: "We are the only socialist country that does not depend upon the Soviet Union." But one day it became known that he was ill with diabetes. He made his way with his Buddha-like body, in a wheelchair, his right pantleg wrinkled following the amputation. He advanced with his cynical smile, his perfect teeth. Until the end, he posed for photos alongside his wife, Jovanka, brandishing a shotgun in Brno Castle. When asked why he lived amidst so much luxury, his would respond: "None of this is mine, it belongs to the Yugoslavian people."

Yugoslavia Kaput.

"Let's go, the air is thinning in this chamber." We creep through the fine sand of the rocks.

## Fifth Circle

"Come along the edge, let's find a path that a person can climb. You first, I will follow you."

On the surface, cemeteries invade everything: soccer stadiums, hillsides, the patios of homes. Tourist hotels were occupied as shelters and centers for international journalists. I visited the Holiday Inn building with yellow mosaic tiles, whose images have been seen by the world. It had a dismal lobby, and I drank a tasteless Turkish coffee where once there was an immense crystal chandelier with glimmering pendants. I climbed the stairs to see the upper stories that were perforated with gaping holes. While I was there, a small electric lightbulb flickered on and off. In this hotel Juan Goytisolo

stayed while he wrote *Sarajevo Notebook*, as did Susan Sontag when she went to stage Samuel Beckett's *Waiting for Godot* by candlelight amidst the bombings. Vladimir and Estragón wait for Godot. Who is Godot? The European Union? NATO? President Clinton?

In the afternoons I would often cross the Miljacka River, observing its crystalline water. In the riverbed a couple of cranes slowly removed debris. I often arrived at the synagogue, in the Jewish quarter, a rose-colored building with the six-pointed star above the window ledges and four ochre-colored domes. Once there, I remembered having read the words in Ladino of the head of the community during wartime, addressing a Spanish newspaper: "I am Bosnian, I am Jewish, and I am Spanish. The savages there above shoot indiscriminately. They kill us because we live together, and we want to continue living together. The idea of an Islamic threat is a fabrication on the part of Milošević. The real fanatics are he and his followers."

Sometimes I stayed for the Shabbat service and left in the middle of prayers in a Hebrew full of "z's". I was accustomed to crossing the same bridge in direction of the Hebrew pharmacy, Apoteka, where I bought medicine. Once, upon climbing the steep slope that leads from the Miljacka River to the cemetery of the Sephardic Jews from Sarajevo, I saw graves with Hebrew letters and stars of David, the dates recent.

## Sixth Circle

"You should refuse all assistance. Some souls cry, stretched out on the ground, face down, but they are not trustworthy."

I place my attention upon the shadows, listening to them cry. We walk among silhouettes of sunken eyes, emaciated faces. Camped there are rusty trains with the doors open. Advancing, descending in circles. We make our way among narrow walls. I want to extract a story from the quarry of the tunnel and follow the vein of its stones. I try to not lose the thread and I become accustomed to seeing out of focus. In some instant, I see myself stretched out with a shroud.

We sit down to rest, hoping that the cloud of smoke clears.

When we meet, he draws near with his grooved fingertips and offers me water. Thirst should fit in the cup of the hand. At times I feel like we are but one person. We advance surrounded by a constellation of drunken fireflies. I see a hole that twists like an arch and embraces all the meadow. According to what the guide says, water falls from one circle to another.

"I had never seen anything like that, it is a new tomb. I don't know how we will get out of here."

Edis pronounces the omitted word and within me I feel a collapse of the galleries. Integral zones of mine become flooded. The dust installed in the forgotten dates of the concentration camps of Koprivnica is stirred, as well as the common grave in which, it is said, my grandfather's body was heaped upon others. I imagine the undifferentiated figures, the shining backsides, the teeth chattering with fear. An execution after being transferred from the jails and hospitals, an August morning in Zagreb. I do not come to leave ashes, rather to search for them in the hills of the north of Maksimir Park. Perhaps by way of the tunnel I may arrive at his grave and recuperate his body. I extend my arm, I touch beyond the surface, I submerge my hand, I think that I am reaching that which is beyond time.

> With Edis we rehearsed our death.
> Each one descends to his tomb.
> We fall onto an earthen bed.

We stretch out in our own hole.
Night enfolds among us.
We lie on our sides in a crouching position, as if we were about to be born.
April, the month of the German bombing of Sarajevo.
April of 1941, April, a thousand bombs.

The letter that I recovered from a family file quotes the threats of the officials at the entrance to the house. I imagine the wide door of the apartment on Maršal Tito Avenue and the military growl:

"Ma'am, if you don't leave this country, the next victims will be your ten-year-old twins. Perhaps, if you baptize your Orthodox children in the Catholic faith, we will pardon them."

On June 25, 1991, the Croatian Parliament (*Hrvatski Državni Sabor*) proclaimed the separation of Croatia from Yugoslavia and declared its independence and sovereignty. Fifteen thousand kilometers away the Yugoslavian Stadium, situated in the Santiago neighborhood of Vitacura, was reinaugurated as the Croatian Stadium. Five percent of the Serbians, we included, were expulsed. We had been members for thirty years. Where would we go in the summer? Goodbye to the Olympic pool with the celeste blue high dive, and to the tree trunks painted with a white band to disorient the ants. Shame and fear prevented us from doing anything and we renounced our membership without protest.

My family was divided in two: those who defined themselves as Croatians and those who defined themselves as Serbians.

The excessive correction or consciousness of "the former Yugoslavia" was now transformed into Yugonostalgia.

## Seventh Circle

"It's time to return, as there is no longer an exit at the airport."

Our feet continue sinking in the mud. We advance the last meters amidst the trickling of the lights and the stalactites. The shutters of the lanterns open, we find ourselves against a backlight. We converse with our eyes half-closed. We advance by force of the light, listening to the terrestrial rumbling. Shovels dig, in the distance the sharpening of knives lurks in the vicinity. We arrive at the end

*The Scents of Memories*

of the tunnel. Together we have poked around the tapestry of history. I'm fatigued, I feel asphyxiated because of the narrow space. I have difficulties breathing, my heart beats faster. Edis repeatedly tells me: "Don't give up." He promises me a sumptuous dinner if I persevere. I draw a deep breath and find strength.

We must contrive secret passages towards the open sky. Return by way of the insane path searching for a glimpse of skylight. Advance by looking upward, gazing down. We ascend, he goes first, and I follow until the sky is a black hole. We have come full circle. While I advance, I begin to lose the prayer like posture. My body acquires height, loftiness, delirium. Edis comes to me and, in the voice of an aged gentleman: "Squeeze your arms tight." He pulls my hand and I climb out, totally covered in mud, head to toe.

> From the depths of the tunnel, I sculpt my new human form.
> I think that this precise moment belongs to me.
> The sky, above; the earthly realm, below.
> Earth, rock, digging and gathering.

There was a lightning bolt of glances in the midst of the light from the yard covered with nettles. The clamps were removed from our eyes, and we gazed at each other. Edis and I are a single figure that defies the well. Silently we advance. Each footstep closes with a seal on all of the paradises promised. We exit to contemplate the stars of the emerging night. His grandparents, Šida and Alija, have placed a winepress in the garage, along with a fire pit. We speak of free windows while we dine on lamb and drink a liqueur made of prunes.

They serve us glass after glass of šljivovica and we toast—*Živeli, živeli* (To your health, to your health)—until the sky ceases to see us.

> Perhaps one would have to learn to decipher
> the anthropology of waste in order to read
> the message of debris.

# The Portuguese Synagogue

*Angelina Muñiz Huberman*

In Amsterdam the words "Violence has a certain unity of form" suddenly came to me.

* * *

In Amsterdam I left the others and walked to the Portuguese synagogue. As if fulfilling a promise. As if seeking solitude: the nostalgia of a place. A place that can only be the center of the universe.

* * *

There with the enormous iron candelabrum in the ceiling: that was the exact spot. Where all acts converge. Where such an appointment with destiny is undeniable.

* * *

You cannot put off what you know is to happen. What else am I doing in the synagogue but waiting for the encounter?

* * *

Sitting on the bench of dark, dense wood. Polished by centuries of clothes rubbing against it. (No one sits down anymore. The visitors stick their heads in quickly and disappear.) (I do sit. I've been sitting for quite some time. So much time that the caretaker grows suspicious. He doesn't know what he suspects, but he suspects something just the same.)

* * *

I run my fingers along the smooth wood. I rest. I hear the sounds of the full synagogue. Packed with recent arrivals from Spain and Portugal. After the edict of expulsion.

* * *

## FRAGMENTED GEOGRAPHIES

What would have occurred during the Nazi occupation? Silence. Silence. Silence. After all the windows and the urns were broken, one by one. Shattered, smashed to bits, crushed to pieces.

* * *

Etty Hillesum walked near the Portuguese synagogue before joining the condemned.

The appointment was sacred.

* * *

What are the sounds I hear? Those of half a millennium ago, or those of forty, fifty years ago?

Both.

* * *

Etty Hillesum approached God in her own way. But her confusion was great. She didn't know what to do with the evil of the world.

She decided to accept chaos.

To wound herself in order to become part of the nightmare.

* * *

Where I am sitting another "I" could have been sitting. One of those women who emigrated and attended the inauguration of the *esnoga* in 1614.

Things can happen or they can not happen.

Here, in the silence of an unvisited temple, the emptiness of God remains. Those who fled the Inquisition found their place and prayed. No one could flee the Nazis.

Two diaries, among others, remained, that of a girl and that of a young woman: Anne Frank and Etty Hillesum. Both interrupted.

I would rather be the woman who sat here centuries ago. Because Anne and Etty are too near. They scratch and tear at me.

That's not true. I wouldn't have wanted to be here in 1614 either. I wouldn't have ever wanted to be in any temple or in any other house of God. And yet, here I am, sitting in the Portuguese synagogue, an empty museum.

I'm the one who's empty.

\* \* \*

I no longer have a time in which to live. History has shattered me. I do not believe. I do not think. I do not feel.

And what's worse: I'm not even an automaton.

And the appalling part: I still possess a weak moral code.

If I have no time, it's because I have no place.

\* \* \*

I probably shouldn't stay in the synagogue. The caretaker is so anxious and so eager for me to leave that when all is said and done he will have his way. Because what am I doing here?

I am just occupying a small section of a long bench made of solid wood. I have installed myself here and I'm not going to move.

I'm beginning to feel my muscles relax, to feel a laziness, a forgetfulness. As if my body were merging with the wood. As if I were no longer myself. As if I had ceased to exist.

I float and am transported.

I could pass through the glass and become part of the blueness of the sky. The iron bars framing the air prevent me from escaping.

Would the victims have escaped this way?

From the prisons of the Inquisition, from the boxcars, from the barbed wire?

No.

No one escaped.

The executioners escaped.

\* \* \*

Although she was a girl, Anne was more mature than Etty. I don't know that for a fact.

Etty was still deceiving herself. She clung to prayers and poetry. To let herself finally be dragged down the path of denial.

\* \* \*

Is it true that she tried to pray in the closed Portuguese synagogue?

\* \* \*

She could still believe. I no longer can.

Despite the presence of the sacred enclosure: a monument to the divine absence.

\* \* \*

I had drawn away from the others: from those who run down the streets, through the museums. And, of course, who pedal their shiny bicycles.

In order to rest in the simple light of the synagogue.

And to take flight.

\* \* \*

Images captivate me, and from them I get my ideas. From glass and mirrors (even those veiled by black cloth). From kaleidoscopes and from stained glass windows.

\* \* \*

Even though I confuse my memory with the memory of others. Did it happen to you or did it happen to me? Is it your memory or mine?

\* \* \*

I don't know my limits very well either. I don't know where I begin and where I am the others. I surprise myself with an imitated gesture, with a word belonging to someone else.

I go from one mimesis to the next.

So, I don't know who I am. I just am. One of these possibilities. Nothing that can be concrete. A sketch of a person. Ambiguous, half-traced.

Ah, but it bothers me that they might recognize in me something that is not mine. After all, it's robbery.

Etty aspired to mystical perfection. I can't believe in it. In the midst of the horror, she became as transparent as air.

When she was able to escape, when it was still possible, she avoided it. She said: if my people die, I will die with them. She didn't want to be a survivor or a witness.

\* \* \*

She thought to leave a final testimony: squeezed together with the hundreds of Jews who were going to meet their death, through some crack in the moving train she threw out a card on which she had written: "We go singing to the concentration camp."

\* \* \*

But I don't accept it. Today, in this temple of so many tears, I don't accept going off to death singing.
 Because it was not a chosen death.
 It was an imposed death. Violence on a whim.
 Agony in the name of fun. Blood spat out.
 The body carried to new depths. The naked scorned.
 The soul slashed.

\* \* \*

And yet, in the abandoned synagogue there is peace. Prayers are still suspended. In the air.

\* \* \*

It's silence.
 What else can it be?
 Silence.

\* \* \*

In the Portuguese synagogue in Amsterdam there are no walls. The space is as vast as the heavenly dome.

\* \* \*

Destruction is present.
    The end of the world is hanging.
    The armies of darkness polish their high, black boots.

\* \* \*

The polished, black boot comes down hard on the bare foot.

\* \* \*

The soldiers' excrement spreads over the roundness of the earth.

\* \* \*

The perfection of the circle is lost.

\* \* \*

The Portuguese synagogue of Amsterdam remains.

\* \* \*

Those who desecrated humanity desecrated themselves first.

\* \* \*

They were the ones who swallowed their own vomit.

\* \* \*

From the shit they proclaimed purity.

\* \* \*

Etty was easily deceived.
    Anne saw the truth.

\* \* \*

With a faint breath, both of them shook the paper army.

\* \* \*

In the synagogue I want to explain the unexplainable. To reason out the unreasonable.

An invented existence could be so peaceful. Simply to let life go where it ought to go. Follow the natural order of things. Instead of having lived this wretched present moment, to resign myself to imagination.

Not to compare. To choose total separation from reality. And thus, to erase history. No issues, no anecdotes. To sink into the flow of mental images. To turn out the light forever. To turn on the darkness.

Since language doesn't serve to explain. Since the word has been broken. Since systems and institutions are hollow scarecrows. Since the ten just men are nowhere to be found. To what heaven do I rise?

\* \* \*

To the one creating the rupture?

\* \* \*

From chaos, what can arise?

\* \* \*

It's true that I drew away from the others. From those who were traveling with me. From those who are still babbling.

And I sat down here, in the Portuguese synagogue. For such a long time. Such a painful time. To think that one day I would think again, that one day I would understand.

That light would begin to shine in my darkness.

That, like the mystics, I would be granted a revelation.

So that just that idea might endure: I would write on black paper one dark night.

\* \* \*

What a desperate coming and going. Gropingly. With the walls receding. Blindly. With the tips of my fingers not feeling a thing.

\* \* \*

To think it is possible to embrace the whole world in this warm space of precious woods that is the Portuguese synagogue of Amsterdam.

\* \* \*

Amen.

# Part II

# In Search of a Lost World

# Jerusalem Is a City on a Hill

*Mimoza Erebara*

Jerusalem is a city-hill of ashes
All of gold and wrapped in gold,
in it walk only people that see God,
the priests, all unseen majesty
like a moon marked full of holiness
Run among the blooming hills
and smell the scattered stones
like the bones that sing in the valley of Ezekiel
where the incense of life will fill your nostrils
will empty your mind, and you will prophesy

"A stone and a stone make a house,
a house and a house, twinkle a suburb"
—this is how I build Jerusalem.

Jerusalem is a city of hills
in those hills there are foreign villages where you get lost
eagle's nests in the rock like edifice
and Jerusalem is a dove among them
that hums sweetly in the mornings in the streets

Did you smell the corpses of Kedar's children
when they gathered in their tribes?
The eagle is upon thee, Jerusalem of gold
the viper is on you
Gazelle among the nations!
Gazelle of Zion!
They conspired
to pluck your shining horns.

# Prisoners

*Luljeta Lleshanaku*

guilty or not
always look the same when they are released—
patriarchs dethroned.

This one just passed through the gate
head bowed despite not being tall
his gestures like a Bedouin's
entering the tent
he carried on his back all day long.

Cotton curtains, stone walls, the smell of burnt lime
take him back to the moment
the cold war ended.

The other day his sheet was hung up in the courtyard
as if to flaunt the blood stain
after a wedding night.

Faces tarnished by sun
surround him, all eyes and ears:
"What did you dream of last night?"
A prisoner's dreams
are parchment
made sacred by its missing passages.

His sister is still discovering his odd habits:
the bits of bread hidden in pockets and under his bed
the relentless chopping of wood for winter.

Why this fear?
What can be worse than life in prison?

Having choices
but being unable to choose.

## Old People's House

A rusty-coloured gate, no name,
The passage to the old people's home.

Amidst the stones in the yard
The grass has withered
Under the weight of many canes.

Behind the curtains, on the windowsills
Dentures float
In water glasses here and there,
Like messages in bottles bobbing on the high sea
Never to be read.

The gate to the old people's home,
Bearing two sad numbers
Is always opened in silence
And hesitation
Like the Bible's much-thumbed pages.

# Amidah: The Silent Prayer

*Entela Kasi*

She was silent and dressed into light
Within the lightning candle she would go to the shepherd
She always called him – my lord
And he always called her – my lady
Her hair was as a crown of harvested grain
Around her beautiful head
On the starry lights
He had a cap on his had
Always black
On Friday nights it was white
Now is time to talk in silence
To listen to our songs
Our land is made of milk and honey
Take the apples from your grandma hands
Don't disturb my lady
Now is time to talk in silence
Three sounds of three broken times

# Silence

*Rita Gabbai-Simantov*

Where are you going, man,
lost in the streets
of old Saloniki?
Neither those neighbourhoods
nor courtyards
nor storytelling on the Sabbath
exist any longer.
As you walk, your companion
will be silence.


# Pretty Salonican Girls

Pretty Salonican girls
Beloved of their mothers:
Seen you full of life
With so much hope
For the days to come,
Who could have imagined
That a cruel power
Would close
Your beautiful eyes for ever
With no hope of seeing the light.

# Part III

# What Our Grandmothers Knew

# It All Started in My Grandparents' Pantry
## Interview with Ivana Vučina Simović

*Jelena Filipović*

## Prologue

Ivana and I have worked together, first as professor and student, then as colleagues, for over twenty-five years now. We've published papers and books on Sephardic sociolinguistics together, we've traveled together, shared our family and personal life stories. I have known about Ivana's Sephardic roots and have encouraged her to start researching topics that in her case are not only relevant to the Hispanic academic community – especially in the Balkans, but also to her personally.

Ivana just needed a little encouragement when she was still an undergraduate student taking my Spanish language and linguistics classes; at a very young age, she began to define her own research interests and spread her academic wings.

As this interview will demonstrate, Ivana was uncomfortable discussing herself. I think it will be clear to our audience why, and they will be the more grateful for this special chance to learn more about the Balkan Sephardim from the varied viewpoints of a Jewish granddaughter, daughter, niece, and scholar and writer.

**Jelena**: Why was it so difficult for you to decide to give me this interview?

**Ivana**: I've never given an interview before. I have never, so to speak, been on this side of the interview table. But now, as the generations of Holocaust survivors begin to leave our earth, I feel more and more that the time has come for me to begin sharing my tale since, before long, there won't be anyone here to do so. I've recently come to see this thought as a sense of obligation – the obligation to discuss the Holocaust. There have been several attempts over the years to refute the historical reality that the Holocaust occurred. I see a relativization of history. I now realize that the significance of preserving the memory can only be fully appreciated by individuals whose identities and families have been molded by these awful historical events. We must therefore keep conversing and sharing our individual tales. I have a feeling that I shall be narrating my story for a longer and longer time from now on. I had steered clear of this for years in an effort to distance myself from the widespread trauma of World War II.

I chose to undertake this interview for that reason. I've come to understand that elder generations who were raised during World War II were trained not to discuss their trauma with others. Both their parents and they themselves believed that being silent would protect them. We now understand better: trauma is passed down through generations. Refusing to discuss it with your kids won't make it go away or disappear. I'm a real-life illustration of this. Naturally, those who survive are the most impacted, but the generations that come after are also severely traumatized.

I shall present you with a fractured family history, as that is how it is organized in my memory. The majority of the information I will discuss in this interview comes from my grandpa, who used to offer me "small portions" of the good and the terrible from his own, his family's, and his Sephardic community's past. My story, then, is akin to a puzzle that I had to piece together for myself as a child while spending time with him and listening to his stories.

### It all started in my grandparents' pantry

*Jelena*: Ivana, can you tell me a bit about how you learned about your Jewish heritage?

*Ivana*: It all started in my grandparents' pantry when I was about ten. Grownups in my family protected the children by not talking about the past, trying to spare us from the trauma of their memories of the Holocaust. Much later, many years later, I realized that you cannot escape the trauma, it emerges in different shapes and forms and at different times. When I was little, I practically did not know anything about my family history. As practically every child, the more I was kept in the dark, the more curious I became.

My cousin on my mother's side, two years older, approached me in my grandparents' pantry one day when I was about ten years old, and told me that our grandmom, my mom's mother, was not my real grandmother, that she was her grandmother only. I was utterly taken aback. I struggled to comprehend what she was trying to tell me. She dropped hints here and there, because she knew more, because the topic of the Holocaust was discussed in her Subotica household. She was older and felt smarter, sharing this new information with me, trying to show me how innocent and uniformed I was. She was not trying to be cruel, just superior in age and knowledge. That moment marked the beginning of piecing together my family life's puzzle. I kept silent for a very long time, I did not mention anything to anybody, not to my parents, not to my grandparents, not to my older sister.

Some time passed by, and one day, I arrive to my grandparents' house and they were acting weird – urging me to sit, offering drinks and sweets, displaying great care and attention. It turned out that they had decided it was time to disclose the truth but were unsure how to broach the subject. At twelve years old, they deemed me mature enough and felt sufficient time has passed from the end of the World War II so that they story could be shared with me. I realized that they were about to tell me. I sat down and tried to figure out how to react since I already knew. As they prepared to share, I sat contemplating how to react, already privy to the information. Their approach was so delicate, and all that time I focused solely on feigning surprise.

And so it went. Even after we talked, I felt that many details were still missing from my family history puzzle. The point of that first conversation was to let me know that my grandmom was my mom's stepmother. That was very difficult for them to tell me. They never mentioned anything about the concentration camp, never mentioned any particular pieces of information. That was all I knew until my grandmother passed away.

### My grandfather – an expert storyteller

*Ivana*: My grandfather was a widower for a long time, and we got along splendidly, I started visiting him on a regular basis. I was with him practically every day and he started sharing vignettes about his life with me. He opened to me, he was the only one talking – my mom has not talked about her early childhood. I supposed they all took it from my grandmom, who believed she had been protecting us by keeping silent, so everybody simply followed her example. It was my grandfather who started unveiling the past. On one hand, he talked a lot about the pre-war times, about his life and adventures. He loved talking about himself, he was always the protagonist of his narratives, and through those stories he started sharing the information with me in small portions. Of course, the other members of his family in Sarajevo were naturally included in his stories.

However, his recollections primarily centered on his time spent in a prisoner of war (POW) camp. Consequently, he would often shift between different time periods – reminiscing about the camp, his life in Sarajevo, his father's professional activities, and his own employment. I began to jot down notes in a small notebook, and years later, on rediscovering it, the patterns in his storytelling became more evident to me. He would share bits of his past during our brief half-hour or 45-minute visits, leaving me to piece together the narrative on my own. While my mother remained silent, I started uncovering the truths hidden within his tales, gradually learning more details. It all began with narratives about the Jewish prisoners, members of the Yugoslav Royal Army in a POW camp where he spent most of the war years. The Jews there were segregated but managed to survive under the protection of the Geneva Convention. He recounted a story of a prisoner who clandestinely passed a list of Jewish POWs to the Red Cross, resulting in his execution, yet ensuring the protection of the others until the war's conclusion. My grandfather used to point out how fortunate it was that *Wehrmacht* and *Gestapo* could not reach an agreement regarding the Jewish prisoners of war which ultimately safeguarded them until the war ended.

Then the history of my mother became clear. He discussed Djakovo, a camp for women and children located close to Osijek, an independent state in Croatia that was a Nazi satellite state. My mother and grandmother from Sarajevo, which was also ruled by the Nazi Croatian government, were among the Jewish women and children transported there from all over the Independent State of Croatia. Several of my grandfather's nine siblings were female Sarajevo relatives who were housed at the camp. Thus, he liked to boast about how Queen Marija had given humanitarian help to the Yugoslav warriors in the POW camp, how he had sold chocolates and cigarettes, and how he had made slippers from old blankets and the story of how he sent money to the family in Osijek that had hidden my mother, and to his sister and her husband in Italy, whose more permissive policies towards the Jews had allowed them to avoid being arrested by the Nazis. My mother was smuggled out of the camp by my biological grandmother, who used her contacts with the Jewish community in Osijek to her advantage as soon as she recognized the end was near. My grandfather used to tell me about my mother, who was a tiny baby due to her premature birth. He enjoyed telling me how she slept in a drawer heated by warmed bricks in a makeshift incubator. He then pauses and switches to a different subject. He then tells me yet again about the Italian Catholic church where his sister played the organ. He used to send money there too, and they would return the favor by sending him food, and so on. My grandfather was delighted to tell me about a series of events that demonstrated his extraordinary ability to survive in any situation. Occasionally, as he told me those stories, he mentioned the details that were left unsaid. I discovered that my grandmother had died either in Djakovo or Auschwitz, but he claimed that he never could have learned about the specifics of her tragic fate. As I began my research in Sephardic studies, I discovered that there were lists of names and that not everything was undocumented, that there is a chance that he had been hiding the facts that he had thought would hurt me the most.

There were further tales regarding my step-grandmother's family as well as mine. There is one excellent example of unspoken truths: One year I was together with my grandparents on the commemoration day of the Novi Sad massacre of Jews, Serbs and Roma under the Hungarian Nazi regime (January 21-23, 1942), and the TV news featured a commemorative piece about it. There, according to my step-grandmother, her entire family had been slain. And that's when we all began to consider that awful incident with even greater seriousness. She was saved because she was married to a Bunjevac, an ethnic Croatian who lived in Vojvodina and was forced to convert to Catholicism. But years later, when I began looking into the family history independently, I discovered that her whole family had been executed in Auschwitz, not in Novi Sad! As if one method of dying is less horrific than another, my step-grandmother found it difficult to even bring up the topic of Auschwitz due to its painful connotations. Instead, she found it simpler to discuss the Novi Sad tragedy!

Every now and then, my mother would also talk about her grandmother – my great-grandmother, who lived to be 93 years old. She kept on claiming her to be the fastest potato peeler who had worked in a canning factory during World War II. I continued thinking that I was a bad person for not knowing how to peel potatoes properly, only to discover on my own (much later in life) that she had also been detained at Auschwitz. Only, she was more fortunate than most. So, my whole childhood and adolescence, I lived not knowing the worst.

*Jelena*: How did you get interested in the Sephardic life in older times (before 1941)?

*Ivana*: Like I said, I really liked my grandfather's stories – he also used to talk a lot about his Sephardic background in Sarajevo, even though his focus was mainly on loss of life and family members (I gradually realized that most of the people he had mentioned did not make it through the war). For instance, he claimed to have lost his original tongue, Judeo-Spanish, which piqued my curiosity as to the roots of the Sephardic migrations. My Sarajevo Sephardic family used to be bilingual until the start of World War II (using Serbian with their siblings, friends, and spouses, and Judeo-Spanish/*Judezmo* with their parents' and grandparents' generations). At the time, I was not a sociolinguist, so I accepted his statements for facts – not thinking about how difficult it would be to forget one's first language after using it for first twenty or more years. I began studying Spanish to honor my granddad. He also explained to we were Sephardim, the descendants of the Jews who were driven from Spain during the Middle Ages. He also told me that not all the Jews are the same – something that I had been aware from the beginning since both my natural grandmother and my step-grandmother were Ashkenazi from Subotica in northern Serbia.

When I began studying Spanish at the age of thirteen, other kids in my school would point fingers at me, saying things like, "This is the girl who studies Spanish," because the language was not as common then as it is now. At that time, no one was aware of the Sephardim.

***Jelena***: What is your mom's relationship to Sephardic traditions? How did she react when you started working in Sephardic studies?

***Ivana***: My mother has always believed in the socialist justice and equality in the best possible way, and she never thought that religious or ethnic backgrounds mattered. Although her name is Rahela, which is a common Jewish name, she did not feel unique or distinct growing up in Sarajevo and Belgrade because there were other Jews living in the neighborhood. Lela is my mom's nickname. Later, when I began conducting independent research, I looked for her religious birth certificate in Sarajevo and saw that Rahela – Lela appears on it; so, her nickname appears to be part of her "official" name. That was a very common occurrence in Sephardic families; many families shared the same last name, like ours, Kampos, though our family was not related to any of them; the children were given the names of their parents and grandparents, so they had to use nicknames to identify individuals and families.

My mother has always been happy knowing that I am a scholar in Sephardic studies and that I have a keen interest in the past of Sephardic communities and in Sephardic women in particular. However, I am far more knowledgeable than she is now because I am the one who has saved my grandfather's numerous stories —he lived to be ninety–giving us plenty of time to piece together the past and for me to forge my own identity. My mother was born in 1940, and she has claimed not to remember anything until her father arrived in Osijek (Croatia) to pick her up. My grandfather left the POW camp and returned to Yugoslavia, where he joined the partisans and pursued her after the war was formally declared over. He already had known what she looked like as the people who took care of my mom were sending her photos to the POW camp. After being smuggled out of the Djakovo camp for women and children, she was originally cared for by a distant relative, an aunt who was married to a Croat. After a year or so, the couple was taken into custody and put to death for listening to British radio broadcasts. My mother was spared from this fate because a neighbor informed the Ustaše that she was actually the child of a Yugoslav officer and not their kid, making no mention of the "Jewish part" of the family. Until the conclusion of the war, the neighbor kept her. That was one more tale from my granddad. My grandfather used to say that my mother spoke fluent German when he came to get her. Later in life, she forgot it, yet she still comprehends everything. She's still curious about how that came to be. My mother likes to recount how her father's beard tickled her when he kissed her when he came for her. He gave her some watercolors, and although she enjoys talking about it, her recollections are highly private, she never shares anything about the "grand narrative of war," and I'm not sure how much of it she truly knows – I'm sure she does, but she won't discuss it.

*Jelena*: and how about your Sephardic Identity? How do you identify yourself in everyday conversations?

***Ivana***: It is very difficult for me to offer a singular definition. My mom is half Sephardic, half Ashkenazi. It's interesting to note that my step-grandmother was the best friend of my real grandmother (they were both from Ashkenazi families in Subotica). During a summer vacation by the sea, my grandfather first got to know my step-grandmother, who then sent my true grandma to Sarajevo to meet my grandfather. Sort of like a movie plot. After they were married, my grandma stayed in Sarajevo. When the war ended and she learned that her best friend had died in war, my step-grandmother set out to find my mother to adopt her, believing that my grandfather would undoubtedly remarry.

I dislike having to define who I am. I have several facets to who I am. My father is Slovenian, born and raised in Belgrade. My spouse is an Orthodox Serbian. I find it easy to identify with Sephardim when I'm with them, and the same is true with Slovenians, though many find that strange. Some people may think: Look at this woman, she changes from one thing to another in an instant. For a long time, I struggled with what is now called an "identity crisis" since I was unsure of my own classification in our predominantly Serbian Orthodox community. It has always seemed weird to me to have to fit in with everyone around me. Growing up, I never really knew how to put it into words, but I always sensed that there was something unusual about me. Then I understood that there are numerous features related to my family education, everyday customs, cuisine, etc. Not much, but you begin to pick up on the difference. Take the refrigerator drawer where we store the veggies, which we refer to as *gemize* (*Gemüse* in German). German borrowings are widespread in my family because they originate from all of our backgrounds: Ashkenazi, Slovenian, and Bosnian Sephardic speakers (because Bosnia was annexed by Austria-Hungary in 1907) all utilized a lot of Germanisms in their daily speech.

***Jelena***: Has it sometimes made you feel uncomfortable or just curious?

***Ivana***: Actually, both. But mostly intrigued. My curiosity has always been piqued, and I found great pleasure in my grandfather's stories, which he shared exclusively with me. For example, we went to Israel together while I was still in high school. My step-grandmother had recently passed away when he made the decision that my aunt should return to Yugoslavia to live with him. I saw and learned so many new things then. Suddenly, I perceived my grandfather in an entirely different light. My grandfather's generation was still living and well established in Israel at the time. There are numerous Sarajevo-born Sephardic families in Israel. Altogether, there were a lot of visits from elderly women who would gaze at him with innocent eyes and then promptly forget a hat or an item of clothing in my aunt's apartment, just to find an excuse to come back. My grandfather, whose nickname was *Lindo* ("handsome" in Judeo-Spanish/*Judezmo*), turned out to be quite the handsome man when he was younger. As a result, he felt like the most popular guy in the neighborhood once more when he was in Israel. I listened while he spoke to them about the past. Every narrative he created, he was able to turn himself into the main character. For instance, my grandfather was a cavalry officer in reserve in the Yugoslav Royal Army. And although he was a little pretentious, I thought all of his stories about him riding a white horse were hilarious and I loved hearing them. Also, I discovered somewhere along the line, that he had four wives! He used to say it was an accident. The first was a ballet dancer he swiftly divorced because she didn't want kids. Six months after they were married, the second one, an Ashkenazi Jew from Czechoslovakia filed for divorce after she got Yugoslav citizenship. My step-grandmother was the final one, of course, and my true grandma was the third. Upon telling my parents about it after our return from Israel, I discovered that my mother was well aware of it, even though my dad had not been informed. One of our old jokes about it was, "They did not tell me in order not to give me any ideas!"

## Sephardic women writers and Ivana's story

**Jelena**: As you've already mentioned, forming your Sephardic identity has been greatly influenced by the Jewish women writers from Belgrade you have come to know and like and be friends with.

**Ivana**: When Gordana Kuić released her debut book, *The Scent of Rain in the Balkans*, in the middle of the 1980s, the general public's understanding of the Sephardim greatly improved. Her narrative fascinated me, and my grandfather piqued my curiosity even further by telling me that in that novel, the first of a tetralogy she would write over the next few decades, Gordana very deftly captured the spirit of the Sephardic existence in Sarajevo. He talked about Gordana's mother and sisters, who he knew personally, and how her grandfather worked as my great-grandfather's secretary. In Sarajevo, where my great-grandfather had a sizable bakery and butcher shop, there was a proverb that said, "Your mouth is as big as Kampos' bakery." It was fascinating – characters from Gordana's novel were part of my grandfather's life story.

So, my connection with Jewish female writers in the Balkans is very much real and everlasting.

**Jelena**: And what about Krinka and Drita?

**Ivana**: My cousin who first revealed my Jewish heritage was an ethnomusicology student in Novi Sad. She told me about her graduation project on Sephardic romances when she visited Belgrade one day many years ago. She asked me to go meet this woman who sings the traditional Sephardic (Spanish) songs and I went with her. I got to know Drita Tutunović that way. We went to see her at her lovely home in Senjak, a very quaint district in Belgrade. She had a large terrace, and we spent hours sitting there talking. During that time, my mind was racing with fresh ideas and details I had never heard of. Back then, I was still in high school. She expanded my understanding of Jewish life by sharing experiences with me that went beyond the Holocaust and included language, music, oral literature, and tradition preservation.

Krinka Vidaković's monograph, which was based on her doctoral dissertation (Kultura španskih Jevreja na Jugoslovenskom tlu, XVI–XX vek, Sarajevo: Svjetlost, 1986), was the third moment. That was another eye-opening realization: this is a legitimate scholarly subject, not merely a collection of personal tales from far-off eras. Sephardic studies is a legitimate topic of study! There actually exists a field of research in Sephardic studies!

I used to talk about my family with my good friends Ana Štulić (now a professor of Spanish and Sephardic studies at the University of Bordeaux) and Gorana Zečević (now a professor of Spanish at the University of Kragujevac) when I first started studying Spanish at the university. Then, you mentioned the Sephardim and Judeo-Spanish in the course on the history of Spanish, and we asked you if we could do a term paper on the topic. We began our research once you enthusiastically gave us the go ahead. I wrote an annotated bibliography on Sephardic print, while Ana wrote an annotated bibliography on language study issues. Under the aliases Saruča and Hanuča – the names of two older female characters from a Buki Romano's short story settled in traditional Sephardic neighborhood – we combined those pieces and submitted them to the Belgrade Sephardic community's yearly call for research papers on Jewish topics.

## A researcher is born

*Jelena*: So you were awarded a prize even before you graduated?

*Ivana*: The fact that you came to interview my grandfather inspired me even more. I found it intriguing that you were interested in him and in what he had to say. Aside from that, Gordana, Drita, and Krinka were very helpful in helping me to define my research interests. They revealed the Sephardic world of pre-World War II, a world full of color, happiness, music, and light. All of it was so different from a terrible undertone to my grandfather's recollections; he would always talk about the number and manner of his relatives' and acquaintances' deaths during the Holocaust.

I came to see that the Sephardic life was not only gloomy and challenging; there were moments in time when things were more hopeful and brighter, and I discovered that. I could write about them. I chose my academic foundation in this way – as a natural progression of my private life.

I once conducted an interview with Drita and began by thanking these three women for bringing the history of the Sephardic people to the attention of the general public through their scholarly writings (Krinka), novels (Gordana), storytelling, and singing (Drita). Thanks to them, eventually I could stop having to explain to people what I do for a living (in the strict academic sense) because Gordana's first novel from the 1980s was a bestseller, and all the others were as well. Krinka is the one who started speaking and writing on Sephardic topics to academic audiences worldwide and who showed me that there is an academic field of Sephardic studies. Drita has been able to maintain the common life and family customs that were absent from my grandfather's stories. For me, Drita provided with historical and cultural context for a plethora of Sephardic proverbs and sayings that my grandfather used to spice his conversations with. I also enjoy using proverbs in my regular conversations, which is why I occasionally find it challenging to converse in other languages. That is why I requested that we conduct this interview in Serbian – I have very specific thought and speech patterns and there are nuances that I can only convey in my first language and so I that this particular language choice would add to my narrative's authenticity.

*Jelena*: You recall my excitement when you came over to me. I have long considered Sephardic studies to be a genuinely Balkan Hispanic subject that has not received enough attention from our local and global Hispanic academic communities. You served as my first 'gate keeper' in an anthropological sense – a community member with a personal connection to the topic, highly motivated, and knowledgeable.

***Ivana***: Don't forget, though, that I have never truly felt like I belong in any of the communities I interact with.

***Jelena***: The important thing to convey to our readers, in my opinion, is that there is no need for divisions, separations, and either/or identity claims.

## Balkan identities

***Ivana***: Yes, but in terms of customs and cultural archetypes, for instance, Serbian Orthodoxy in the Balkans is essentially easily defined. In the Balkan Jewish communities, however, diversity is much greater, and it is more difficult to pinpoint aspects of clearly-cut Jewish (Sephardic or Ashkenazi) identity. Unlike in what Paloma Díaz Mas refers to as the 'Secondary Diaspora,' where Jewish people find themselves in settings where there is a different majority, such as Serbs in Chicago, for example, they feel compelled to form their own communities and stick together. In the Balkans, we have lived in in multiethnic societies for centuries. This is not the case with many Jewish communities in the Americas. Notwithstanding their sense of belonging to larger communities, I get the impression that the Jewish identity is much more strongly defined there. Here, heterogeneity is the foundation of all our identities, so I would say that there is a complex identity of the Balkan Jewry. Just take a look at the languages we speak; Judeo-Spanish is just one example of the numerous languages which have been in contact the Balkans for such a long time.

***Jelena***: Could it be that there are two fundamental differences between Jewish identities in the Balkans and Latin America – language and religion? In the Balkans, Jewish identity is more fluid than in other parts of the world due to the diversity of languages and religions. In Latin America, on the one hand, the language made it easier for Sephardim to assimilate; on the other hand, the Jewish religion becomes a differentiating factor when contrasted with a strong Roman Catholic tradition.

***Ivana***: Yes, I've had numerous opportunities to serve as a guide to researchers who come to Belgrade to study the Sephardim, and each time it seemed to me that they had very clear ideas about what they were going to discover. As a result, I found myself trying to point out to them that here nothing is ever as clear as they expect. This is just my opinion; perhaps someone else could provide some other interpretation, but I firmly believe that the boundaries between different identities are hazy in the Balkans. There is also a socialist component to our life in the former Yugoslavia, which made discussing or passing judgment on people's language or religion choices and identities even less pertinent. In former Yugoslavia, we grew up not concerned about being singled out on any account because the socialist society in which we lived was far more benign than in other communist countries. However, the clear-cut identity lines are still drawn at the institutional level. For instance, I still have trouble answering identity questions on official censuses since it is not allowed to check more than one box. For many people living in Serbia, the identity concept is a blurry issue. And officially, identity is supposed to be an either/or category. For some reason people want it to be made simple, yet nothing is ever that easy.

***Jelena***: One possible takeaway from this interview could be that you found your Sephardic identity in an academic context because of your personal background and the need not to be identified with one single group or community.

***Ivana***: Yes, and I have met colleagues and other individuals that have a very distinct Sephardic identity throughout my academic travels, conferences, and visits to various locations in Europe and Israel. Speaking with them gave me more insight into my family's history. Particularly in Israel, where our Sarajevo-born relatives reside. My interest in and understanding of the Sephardic life and customs have grown with each interaction and gathering. In terms of my identity and areas of interest for study, I have established my safe zone, where I am at ease acting as both a scientist and an observer. My intellectual and personal lives have been coexisting;

I'm aware of and actively seek out my comfort zones. For instance, I have never been able to conduct the interviews with Holocaust survivors. Many of the elder generations were still alive when I began my academic life as a researcher, and they had a wealth of insightful things to share. However, that was too near to my own trauma. I now regret it, but at the time I believed that studying the Holocaust would have too much of an impact on my own life. Thus, I decided to conduct archive investigation.

That gave me great satisfaction since it allowed me to learn a lot from the authentic materials I worked with, which frequently date back far further than World War II. Working with written data allows you to put it down and take a break from the subject. However, face-to-face communication is too personal, and I got the impression that I would be exposed to too much information that would have a significant impact on me. With my grandfather, things were different because, in addition to the fact that I loved him dearly, we never had lengthy conversations; instead, his life story was given to me in fragments. He was also an extremely happy, carefree, and successful under any circumstances.

Therefore, science serves as my compass, even though there are, of course, connections between scientific fields of study and my real life. I can't remember who phoned my grandfather after Ana Štulić and I received the award at the Belgrade Jewish community, but they congratulated him on having a granddaughter who is interested and engaged in Sephardic studies. It was a moment of great pride for him. All in all, my family and friends have always responded well to the things I accomplish, which gave me confidence that I've been on the correct track.

I am both here and not here at the same time. Since that day at my grandparents' pantry, I have been exposed to trauma, but I learned to handle it. The intriguing thing is that I am still struggling with my identity in many ways. During our June 2023 round table discussion about Jewish women at the University of Graz, I couldn't help but wonder if I truly fit the profile of a Jewish woman. I had never before discussed my Jewish heritage in public until then. I used to chat to my Serbian friends all the time, and they thought my stories were really exotic and that they were sort of living a movie story line with me. However, each survivor family's experience is a screenplay for a film. I keep thinking that when I occasionally take a look at the tape that contains the interview Spielberg did with my grandfather and a few other people.

And thinking back to Graz, I found it quite awkward to discuss myself with a wider group of people. I was a little anxious as well because I was going outside of my comfort zone when you asked me for this interview. Usually, I'm the one asking questions because I find it difficult to respond to inquiries about my background that are personal. However, you made it simpler for me to speak.

***Jelena***: Even though I've been familiar with the majority of your family's history for a while, I truly liked our talk and the way you were able to share your memories. In addition, I want to express my gratitude to Drita (Tutunović), Gordana (Kuić), and Krinka (Vidaković Petrov) for inspiring you and guiding you through the fascinating realm of Sephardic history. For allowing the light to enter.

# In the End What Remains Are the Words: "A Late Letter to My Grandmother Sali"

*Michal Held Delaroza*

> "To remember / Is to live anew
> *Recordar / Es vivir de nuevo*
> \* \* \*
> I sing your name / I sing the words
> Everything seems to return / To a clear beginning
> *Canto tu nombre / Canto las letras*
> *Todo parece regresar a un / Principio claro*"
> (Marjorie Agosín, Poems for Josefina / *Poemas para Josefina*)[1]

The invitation to participate in a collection of texts by Jewish women writers of the Balkans made me think of my grandmother, who was born in Romania to an Ashkenazi Jewish family. The more I was thinking about her in this context, the more I realized that characterizing her as a Jewish woman of the Balkans is puzzling from many aspects. For example, in addition to its Romanian name, her hometown of Fălticeni, the town situated in the Suceava county of northeastern Romania, has slightly different German, Hungarian, Hebrew, and Yiddish names, and the linguistic variation is a sign of the diverse historical and social experience of the people who called this place their hometown in the historical region of western Moldavia. Languages and linguistic shifts shall reappear in this essay, around a poem I wrote addressing my grandmother. Yet, before we get there, it is worth considering some of the facts that the poem is related to.

---

[1] Translated from the Spanish by Michal Held Delaroza.

According to the *Encyclopedia Britannica* definition of the Balkans, "There is no universal agreement on the region's components [...] Some define the region in cultural and historical terms and others geographically, though there are even different interpretations among historians and geographers".

Geographically, Romania is only partially located on the Balkan peninsula. Socially, culturally, and conceptually, as pointed out by the Romanian historian Sorin Atohi in his essay "Romania and the Balkans," it has experienced cycles of Balkanization, de-Balkanization, and re-Balkanization. Atohi opens his analysis with the claim that "Romanian intellectuals, academics, writers, artists, and politicians have been 'imagining the Balkans,' and have been reflecting on their own ambivalent connections to that part of the world over the past two centuries or so".[2] The Romanian–Balkan enigma is even further complicated when zooming in and trying to think about it in relation to the definition of the Jewish women of the region. However, since the question at stake is one of identity formation, which I have always believed is a dynamic process that cannot and should not be "flattened," my aim in the following discussion is not to solve it, but to accept its complexity while looking at my personal experience as the granddaughter of a Romanian Ashkenazi Jewish woman from Romania from the Balkan perspective.

My grandmother, Haia-Sara Held, whom we called *Savta* (Hebrew for grandma) *Sali*, was born in Romania in 1907, made *aliyah* to Israel at the age of 44 in 1951 and died here in 1985. Growing up a few blocks away from my grandparents, my grandmother was much loved and very present in my childhood and young adult life. Was she a Jewish woman of the Balkans? Am I a Jewish woman of the Balkans being her granddaughter? These questions were never spelled out between the two of us, or in my dialogue with my father, her son, and with other family members who knew her well. Thinking now of Savta Sali, I can detect a sense of retrospective

2   www.iwm.at/transit-online/romania-and-the-balkans (accessed October 1, 2025).

Balkanization (to echo Atohi's terms) as one of the components that intertwined to form our identity.

Identity, however, is made up of fragments, such as the story that my grandmother Sali told me about how (for reasons that she did not elaborate on except for a vague mention of a fire that led to the abandonment of the family house, and I shall always feel frustrated for not asking her to unfold them) as a young girl she fled with her family to Turkey, then still the heart of the Ottoman Empire. The picture that stayed with me from that story is her detailed description of a wall covered with Ottoman-style copper kitchenware and dishes that was the center of the family's temporary Turkish home. In a way that I cannot logically decipher, the senses and smells of the Balkans that were included in her anecdotal Turkish story are more vividly present in my memory than my grandmother's much longer central European Ashkenazi experience. Possibly, this was due to the fact that I intuitively sensed that historically Romania was part of the Ottoman state that formed one space in which Jews moved along the years.

The kitchen of Sali's childhood, unified as it appeared in the story that she told me, connects us to food and to language. Although being an outstanding cook was not one of my grandmother's virtues, the culinary tradition that we did experience in her home most resembled those of the Balkans. Out of her Israeli kitchen came, in their distinctive Jewish Romanian style, the flavors of staffed vine leaves, fried kashkaval cheese, eggplant salads, extensive use of garlic, jam made of rose petals, and walnuts, and maybe most curiously – a sweet humus paste. This last dish is symbolic not only in the fact that it was foreign to the Israeli palate that is used to the Mediterranean savory version of humus, but also in its name, "Nuhut." When my grandmother made it, my father and myself were the only ones in the family to like it, while suspiciously stared at around the table. It never occurred to me to ask about the origin and name of this dish, which I was convinced were simply Romanian. Only recently did I discover that *nuhut* is the Turkish word for "chickpeas," which ties all the strings together and takes us back to the Balkan components of my grandmother's identity that was passed on to me.

The connection between food and language is a powerful identity formation tool, especially in the context of a journey that aims at tracing the deluded Balkan identity of us (maybe) being Jewish women of the Balkans, while creating an intersection between the culinary and the poetic aspects of the process. According to Marjorie Agosín:

> Poetry is a gesture of memory intended to cover absence, an extension of the truth. Poetry requires that they [= the dead] be named and found. Poetry demands to know the whereabouts of oblivion. I write in order to survive. I become their words and my own.[3]

Indeed, working with poetry was the cartographic tool that enabled me to explore, to expose and to define the house of memory whose foundations are, among other experiences, the interaction with my grandmother, Savta Sali. What I am trying to explain to myself here, is the idea that poetry is made of the fragments of memories, which are then re-joined to form a wider structure that is Memory. Marjorie Agosín connected this process to our life-long relationship with the dead, and to the work that we are doing with them through poetry, to avoid oblivion. Those who are familiar with Agosín's own poetic journey, and especially with her three works that are dedicated to her grandmothers,[4] know that she travels extensively around the outer and inner world, and wherever the journey takes her, she very often finds herself going back to her grandmothers and great grandmothers, giving them a voice that shall remain present in the world after them.

As Marjorie Agosín's insight makes clear, in poetry we name and find the dead, becoming their words and our own. Applying this understanding to that of my own experience takes me to the poem

---

3   Marjorie Agosín, *Cartographies: Meditations on Travel,* Athens, Georgia & London 2004, pp. 64-65.
4   Marjorie Agosín, *The Angel of Memory / El angel de la memoria,* Wings Press, 2001. Marjorie Agosín, *Poems for Josefina / Poemas para Josefina,* Sherman Asher, 2004. Marjorie Agosín, *Braided Memories / Memorias trenzadas,* Solis Press, 2020.

about my beloved grandmother Sali, my father's mother, close to whom I grew up. On this journey, my poetic toolbox included more languages than my Hebrew mother tongue, and the layered linguistic variety became the foundation for the house of memory that I constructed and am still constructing. As it happened, I started thinking about this essay and putting the experience into words during the COVID-19 pandemic that secluded everyone around the globe to the limited house-home space. It was when the outer space social space was forbidden and the seemingly limiting house turned into a vast space that invited and encouraged the building of the house–home of memory, that I started thinking of my grandmother in this context.

One of the most tragic effects of the pandemic was the fact that many of its victims, especially the elderly ones, died in quarantined hospital wards, when their loved ones were prevented from giving them the care and farewell that every human being deserves. Years earlier, my grandmother outlived my father, her only son, whose life ended at the age of 49 during the first Lebanon War in 1982, when he volunteered to rejoin the Israeli Defense Forces and defend Israel, the country that he had never left ever since they arrived from Romania when he was seventeen years old. Sali died many years ago, before this pandemic could have been imagined. After the loss of my father, my mother, my sister and myself were the only ray of light in her life. Unfortunately, due to human negligence and blindness, which in a way I find to be even worse than the virus, she died in loneliness at a hospital we were never notified that she had been moved to; we could not say our last farewell to her. Savta Sali, grandmother Sali, kept coming back to me during the pandemic, evoking in me a great sorrow and a deep regret for not accompanying her when she most needed me. This essay is a late letter to her, composed of the fragments of languages that we exchanged during the part of my life I was fortunate to have spent with her and that found their way into a multilingual poem.

Since his arrival to Israel, my father ideologically refused to speak any language other than Hebrew with anybody but his parents, let alone to teach his daughters his mother tongue, which he saw as an obstacle on his way to acquire and fully adapt to Israeli society and culture. Unlike him, my grandmother who never fully mastered the Hebrew language replaced it with an idiolect comprising of a unique combination of all her languages, which may have been unstandardized and improper, but to my ears it was so sweet that it actually became the catalyst for the poem I wrote about her many years later.

The poem's Hebrew (and the English in the mirroring version) is the tapestry on which Romanian words are embroidered, introducing the sounds of the Balkans. Also embedded in the text are Turkish and French words that were interwoven into my grandmother's Romanian and passed on to me as a child, when her newly acquired Israeli Hebrew was not rich enough to fully express herself, and brightened our conversations like sparkling jewels from a faraway reality. I shall not further analyze the poem but rather leave it open for the readers' independent response. I can only share that it was created around the list of those words that Savta Sali was using many years ago. As much as these words were linguistically foreign to me, emotionally they felt very close to the heart because they encapsulated our loving relationship, relating to the semantic fields of the intimate material culture (food, garments, feminine objects) as well as to a wider context of social and cultural life.

I believe that by transferring to me these words as a part of our ongoing dialogue that on her side was carried in a seemingly "broken Hebrew" she has actually bequeathed to me a whole that is larger than the sum of its parts: a sense of continuity, echoing, among other things Romania and the Balkans. One of the lessons of identity creation that I am learning from this dialogue is the realization that the understanding of oneself may be "wholly broken" and does not need to be mended into a flattened definition. In the specific context of the present anthology, I read *Fragmented Geographies* as fragmented identities, believing that we are free to let go of the insistence on the exact definition of Romania as part of the Balkans. For as long as its Balkan nature has a place within my Romanian-born grandmother and myself, Romania has a place on the Balkan peninsula. The following poem that echoes this process is dedicated to Savta Sali as a token of love and gratitude for her inspiration that became a pillar-stone of my house of memory.

## Pour etre belle/To be beautiful

in the end what remains of my grandmother Sali
who came from the Romanian city of Fălticeni to the shocking
onion fields of the **Maabarah** the immigrant absorption camp
in the end what remains of my great love for her
are not the objects she sold back there
candlesticks and jewels
to bring over here down blankets and white enamel pails
with a blue edge

in the end what remains are the words
that are scattered
rolling around
lost in her mouth that never adjusted to Hebrew
"look what I've lost" she said
when finding a treasure
and added "I need a please" instead of a favor - - -

so look what i have found grandmother Sali
in the depths of memory
gleaning words out of the idioms on the shores of which you lived

i who never managed to ride a bicycle
in your Romanian set with the precious stones of French and Turkish
and of Hebrew fragments
in it i fly a **bicicletă**
dressed like a **țigancă** a gypsy girl meeting on the way
a monkey and a parrot
a **papagal** and a **maimuță**
and maybe it was not accidentally that you chose to teach us the names
of these specific animals

so that we repeat after you and get hold of the words that are
all that's left
tied to your bicycle is a suitcase
your **geamantan**
and in it are more words that you had given me
to sweeten the road
**dulceață de trandafiri** rose petals jam
**dulceață de nuci verzi** green walnut jam
**evantai** a folding fan
to lessen the heat
and also a **capac** a decontextualized lid that lost its pot
and that i might find useful for something one day

grandmother Sali was not much of a cook
but when a **musafir** a guest arrived unannounced
she masterfully improvised out of leftovers
a **salată de boeuf** chicken in mayonnaise salad crowned
with a sparkling single black olive
whispering in the kitchen that we shouldn't worry
the guests will eat whatever we put on the table

she knew how to paint reality with the color **lila**
enveloping everything with a light purple cloud and the smell of lilac
that i lost since she was wearing it
while turning a piece of cardboard into a fan
sitting on a stripped **chaise longue**
in the heat of Ramat-Gan reading the Romanian newspaper
**Viața Noastră** Our Life – – –

i cover myself with the down blanket that you brought from Fălticeni
reciting after you
**Pour etre belle il faut soufrir**     One must suffer to be beautiful
**Il faut soufrir pour etre belle**     To be beautiful one must suffer

repeating your words out loud
between the **lila** colored sheets
i am thanking God that one must no longer suffer
nothing but the pleasure of pain
and that of the lover

**P.S.**
it's been years that you are gone and i
repent
that when i helped you button
the bra that you were always strict about
i did not ask
if you suffered to be
Beautiful

## כְּדֵי לִהְיוֹת יָפָה / Pour etre belle

בַּסּוֹף מָה שֶׁנּוֹתַר מִסָּבְתָא סָאלִי
שֶׁבָּאָה מִפְּלִיטִיצָ'ן הַיָּשֵׁר אֶל חֶלֶם הַבֹּצֶל בִּשְׂדוֹת הַמַּעְבָּרָה בְּרִשְׁפּוֹן
בַּסּוֹף מָה שֶׁנּוֹתַר מֵאַהֲבָתִי הַגְּדוֹלָה אֵלֶיהָ הֵם
לֹא הַחֲפָצִים שֶׁמָּכְרָה שָׁם
פְּמוֹטוֹת וְתַכְשִׁיטִים
כְּדֵי לְהָבִיא לְכָאן שְׂמִיכוֹת פּוּךְ וּפְיָלוֹת מֵאֱמַיְל לָבָן
עִם פַּס כָּחֹל

בַּסּוֹף נִשְׁאֲרוּ הַמִּלִּים
הַפְּזוּרוֹת
הַמִּתְגַּלְגְּלוֹת
הָאֲבוּדוֹת בְּפִיהָ שֶׁמֵּעוֹלָם לֹא הִסְתַּגֵּל לְעִבְרִית
"תִּרְאִי מָה חִפַּשְׂתִּי" אָמְרָה
כְּשֶׁמָּצְאָה מְצִיאָה
וְהוֹסִיפָה "יֵשׁ לִי בְּבַקָּשָׁה" – – –

אָז תִּרְאִי מָה חִפַּשְׂתִּי סָבְתָא סָאלִי
בְּנִבְכֵי הַזִּכָּרוֹן
דּוֹלָה אֶת הַמִּלִּים מֵהַשָּׁפוֹת שֶׁעַל גְּדוֹתֵיהֶן חָיִית

אֲנִי שֶׁאַף פַּעַם לֹא הִצְלַחְתִּי לִרְכֹּב עַל אוֹפַנַּיִם
בָּרוֹמָנִית שֶׁלָּךְ שֶׁבְּתוֹכָהּ מְשֻׁבָּצוֹת הַצָּרְפָתִית וְהַטּוּרְקִית
וּבְשִׁבְרֵי הָעִבְרִית
אֲנִי טָסָה עַל bicicletă
לְבוּשָׁה כְּמוֹ țigancă יַלְדָּה צוֹעֲנִיָּה פּוֹגֶשֶׁת בַּדֶּרֶךְ
קוֹף וְתֻכִּי
maimuță וְגַם papagal
וְאוּלַי לֹא בְּמִקְרֶה דַּוְקָא אֵלֶּה הַחַיּוֹת שֶׁלִּמַּדְתְּ אוֹתָנוּ אֶת שְׁמוֹתֵיהֶן
כְּדֵי שֶׁנַּחֲזֹר אַחֲרַיִךְ וְנִתְפֹּס אֶת הַמִּלִּים
שֶׁהֵן כָּל מָה שֶׁנּוֹתַר

לְאוֹפַנַּיִךְ קְשׁוּרָה מִזְוָדָה
הַ-geamantan שֶׁלָּךְ
וּבָהּ עוֹד מִלִּים שֶׁנָּתַתְּ לִי
כְּדֵי לְהַמְתִּיק אֶת הַדֶּרֶךְ
dulceață de trandafiri רִבַּת עֲלֵי וְרָדִים
dulceață de nuci verzi רִבַּת אֱגוֹזִים יְרֻקִּים
evantai מְנִיפָה
כְּדֵי לְהָפִיג אֶת הַחֹם
וְגַם capac מִכְסֶה נָטוּל הֶקְשֵׁר שֶׁאִבֵּד אֶת הַסִּיר
וְשֶׁאוּלַי יוֹם אֶחָד עוֹד יְשַׁמֵּשׁ לִי לְמַשֶּׁהוּ – – –

סָבְתָא סָאלִי לֹא בִּשְּׁלָה מִי־יוֹדֵעַ־מָה
אֲבָל כְּשֶׁהִגִּיעַ musafir אוֹרֵחַ לְלֹא הוֹדָעָה
הִיא הֵיטִיבָה לְאַלְתֵּר מִשְּׁאֵרִיּוֹת
salată de boeuf סָלָט עוֹף בְּמַיּוֹנֵז עִם כֶּתֶר זַיִת שָׁחֹר אֶחָד
בּוֹהֵק בַּמֶּרְכָּז
לוֹחֶשֶׁת בַּמִּטְבָּח שֶׁלֹּא נִדְאַג
הָאוֹרְחִים יֹאכְלוּ כָּל מָה שֶׁנַּנִּיחַ עַל הַשֻּׁלְחָן

הִיא יָדְעָה לִצְבֹּעַ אֶת הַמְּצִיאוּת בְּצֶבַע lila
שֶׁעָטַף הַכֹּל בְּעָנָן סָגֹל בָּהִיר וּבְנִיחוֹחַ הַלֵּילָךְ
שֶׁנֶּעֱלַם לִי
מֵאָז שֶׁלָּבְשָׁה אוֹתוֹ
כְּשֶׁהָפְכָה פִּסַּת קַרְטוֹן לִמְנִיפָה
יוֹשֶׁבֶת עַל chaise longue כִּסֵּא נוֹחַ מִירִיעוֹת פְּלַסְטִיק
בַּחַמְסִין שֶׁל רָמַת גַּן וְקוֹרֵאת בַּ-Viața noastră הָעִתּוֹן הָרוֹמָנִי
אֵלֶּה הֵם חַיֵּינוּ – – –


אֲנִי מִתְכַּסָּה בַּעֲנַן שְׂמִיכַת הַפּוּךְ שֶׁהֵבֵאת מִפְּלֶטִיצֶ'ן
וּמִדְקַלֶּמֶת בְּעִקְבוֹתַיִךְ
Pour etre belle il faut soufrir    כְּדֵי לִהְיוֹת יָפָה צָרִיךְ לִסְבֹּל
Il faut soufrir pour etre belle    צָרִיךְ לִסְבֹּל כְּדֵי לִהְיוֹת יָפָה


חוֹזֶרֶת בְּקוֹל רָם עַל מִלּוֹתַיִךְ
בֵּין הַסְּדִינִים בְּצֶבַע lila
מוֹדָה לָאֵל עַל כָּךְ שֶׁאֵין יוֹתֵר חוֹבָה לִסְבֹּל
אֶלָּא אֶת עֹנֶג הַכְּאֵב
וְעֹנֶג הָאוֹהֵב


נ.ב.
כְּבָר שָׁנִים שֶׁאֵינֵךְ וְשֶׁאֲנִי
מִצְטַעֶרֶת
שֶׁכַּאֲשֶׁר עָזַרְתִּי לָךְ לִסְגֹּר אֶת הַ-sutien
הֶחָזִיָּה שֶׁתָּמִיד הִקְפַּדְתְּ עָלֶיהָ
לֹא שָׁאַלְתִּי
אִם סָבַלְתְּ כְּדֵי לִהְיוֹת
יָפָה

In conclusion, are we – my grandmother and myself – women of the Balkans? Memory and identity are too flexible to provide a clearcut answer, and I believe that the dynamic process of asking this question is more important and valuable than the answer. Romania may be regarded as a Balkan crossroad, neighboring states such as Bulgaria and Serbia and overlooking Turkey across the Black Sea. Culinarily, as already hinted at, it is strongly influenced by the Balkan and Ottoman traditions. Through its traditional music, which provided the source melody of the Israeli anthem *Hatikvah*, Balkan tunes can be heard. Romanian belongs to the family of Romance languages and has Turkish elements embedded in it, which puts it in a linguistic position closer to the Balkans than to the neighboring Slavic languages of central and eastern Europe. However, my grandmother spoke Yiddish alongside with Romanian as a mother tongue, and we both are Israelis by birth and by choice, who were connected by (her broken) and (my confident) Hebrew.

Where does all this take us? To complement the understanding of the Black Sea as representation of the relationship between the Balkan centers that developed at its shores, I am thinking of the Danube River. And the partial conclusion that I can reach while trying to navigate this personal journey of decoding and deciphering our Romanian and Balkan identity, is that although it originates north of the Balkans, the greater part of the Danube's delta lies in Romania, where it flows into the Black Sea. At least metaphorically, then, my grandmother and myself are sharing a fragmented identity that was created in relation to the fragmented geography that lies between Romania and Israel and to that the parts that the countries they are co-playing in the story of our lives. A story with many fragrances and flavors, among which those of the Balkans can sure be sensed and tested.

SALI ON HER WEDDING DAY IN FĂLTICENI, ROMANIA (PHOTO FROM THE HELD FAMILY ARCHIVE).

MY GRANDMOTHER AND MYSELF: SHE LOOKING INTO THE FUTURE; ME PLAYING WITH THE BEADS OF MEMORY (PHOTO FROM THE HELD FAMILY ARCHIVE).

# Editors and Contributors

**Marjorie Agosín** was a Chilean–American poet, human rights activist, and author of numerous books about the Jewish experience in Europe and Latin America. Her creative work was inspired by the pursuit of remembrance and the memorialization of traumatic historical events. She wrote about the Holocaust through the portrayal of Anne Frank, about the history of Bosnian women during the siege of Sarajevo, as well as about the role of women in Latin America during authoritarian regimes. She was a professor of Latin American Literature at Wellesley College, USA, and the winner of numerous literary awards, among which the Letras de Oro and the Latino Literature Prize for poetry. She wrote essays, autobiographical memoirs, and a young adult novel. Her most recent poetry collection, *Braided Memories* (Solis Press, 2020), composed together with photographer Samuel Shats, awakens her great-grandmother, Helena Broder's memory, and her escape from Vienna for Chile.

**Ruth Behar** was born in Havana, grew up in New York, has lived in Spain and Mexico, and returns often to Cuba to build bridges around culture, literature, and art. Her nonfiction books, *Translated Woman, The Vulnerable Observer, An Island Called Home,* and *Traveling Heavy,* have been acclaimed for their mix of personal and ethnographic writing. She is also the author of a bilingual book of poetry, *Everything I Kept/Todo lo que guardé*. Behar won the Pura Belpré Author Award for her coming-of-age-novel, *Lucky Broken Girl*. Her novel *Letters from Cuba*, a work of historical fiction, is based on her grandmother's escape from Poland to start a new life in Cuba on the eve of World War II. She was the first Latina to win a MacArthur "Genius" Grant and has been named a "Great Immigrant" by the Carnegie Corporation. Behar is the Victor Haim Perera Collegiate Professor of Anthropology at the University of Michigan in Ann Arbor.

**Mimoza Erebara** studied at the University of Tirana, Albania, specializing in language and literature. She worked as a journalist and editor for a long time in Albanian newspapers such as *Zëri i rinisë* and *Republika*. She has collaborated with various media outlets in Albania and worldwide. She has published various collections of poetry and short stories in Albanian to great acclaim, and in 2019 an *Anthology of Hebrew Poetry*. Erebara has been published in various literary magazines in Albania and abroad. She has received the Gold Medal for poetry from the European Academy of Arts in Paris, and numerous awards in the country. She holds the title "Ambassador of Peace." Currently, Erebara works as a journalist in the daily press in Tirana.

**Jelena Filipović** is a professor of Spanish and Sociolinguistics at the Department of Iberian Studies at the University of Belgrade. Her research interests are in the areas of critical sociolinguistics, language policy and planning, gender studies, Sephardic studies, Hispanic and applied linguistics. She has authored, co-authored and co-edited thirteen books, and published several dozen academic articles. She has been engaged in a number of national and international projects in the areas of language education policies, collaborative knowledge construction and academic maturation, minority language policy and planning, gender-sensitive language policies, foreign and second language teaching curriculum design and development, and language maintenance and revitalization. She is an international expert of the European Center for Modern Languages and a member of the Board of Education of the Serbian Academy of Sciences and Arts.

**Rita Gabbai-Simantov** was born in Athens, Greece, to a Jewish family of Sephardic origin. In December of 1942, she and her family fled the Nazi-occupied Greece for Turkey, where they lived until the war ended. Judeo-Spanish and traditional religious practice permeated her life in Turkey, as she lived with her grandparents who, unlike her parents, were more scrupulous observers of Judaism and spoke mainly in Ladino. This permeance faded somewhat upon their return to Athens, where she attended a non-Jewish Greek school, and her parents often opted to speak French rather than Ladino at home. Still, language, Judeo-Spanish in particular, remained an important part of her life. Ladino was the preferred language of her husband and his family, and her job at the Israeli Embassy regularly put her in contact with the language and Sephardic culture. Her trip to Spain in 1991 inspired her to begin writing poetry, with her strong self-identification with Sephardic roots making Ladino the most natural linguistic choice. She has since published three anthologies of Ladino poetry: *Quinientos Anios Despues* (1992), *Fuente de mi Tradision* (1999), and *Poezias de mi Vida* (2007). Her poems explore various themes, with the diversity in subject designed to represent more completely the Sephardic diaspora experience.

**Michal Held Delaroza** is a thinker, researcher, poet, and visual artist. Her scholarly work focuses on the Judeo-Spanish (Ladino) culture and literature, and she serves as advisor to the Israeli Authority for Ladino and an *académico correspondiente* of the Real Academia Española. During more than twenty years of lecturing and researching at the Hebrew University, she published numerous academic essays focusing on the Sephardic experience, emphasizing issues of gender, identity, the Sephardic Holocaust, and the digital homeland of the Sephardim. Her book of research is an analysis of the personal narratives of Judeo-Spanish-speaking women storytellers. Recently, she co-edited the Old Sephardi Yishuv in Eretz Israel volume in the Ben Zvi Institute of Jewish Communities in the East series. In her three volumes of poetry, and a fourth one soon to be published, Hebrew is intermingled with Judeo-Spanish and a few other languages. In her visual artistic work, she concentrates on painting, while also experimenting in other art forms, such as mosaics and ceramics, with a special interest in combining and reassembling recycled objects into new creations. On the whole, her work aims at reaching a co-existence of the creative and the scholarly perspectives that do not negate but complement each other, employing interdisciplinary and multi-layered methods.

**Oana Hergenröther** was born to Romanian parents in the northern Serbian province of Vojvodina and has grown up balancing between the two languages and the two, inseparable, aspects of her identity: the Slavic and the Romance. She obtained her PhD in English and American Studies from the University of Novi Sad, adding English as a third inalienable part of her cultural repertoire. Presently, she speaks mostly Spanish, the common language with her German husband, in Austria, where she currently works as a researcher at the University of Graz. Her interests are in literatures in plurilingual and minority contexts, contemporary American literature and culture, intermediality studies, and aging studies. She is the author of a monograph about Paul Auster's work, and outside her academic work an active literary translator and a published author of short fiction.

**Andrea Jeftanovic** born in Santiago de Chile, is a novelist, storyteller, essayist, and professor. Her family is originally from Bulgaria and other parts of the Balkans; around the 1940s, they established themselves in Chile. She is an author of fiction: the novels *Escenario de guerra* and *Geografía de la lengua*, and the short story collections *No aceptes caramelos de extraños* and *Destinos errantes*. All these titles delve into memory, violence, displacement, intimacy. In nonfiction, her books are *Conversaciones con Isidora Aguirre*, *Hablan los hijos*, *Escribir desde el trapecio*. She also writes theater reviews for newspapers and collaborates in literary publications. Her work has received several awards, including the Chilean Art Critics Circle Award, National Book and Reading Council Award, The Pen Translation Prize. Her work has also been translated into several languages and appears in international as well as Chilean anthologies. She completed a PhD in Hispanic Languages and Literatures at the University of California, Berkeley. Currently, she is full Professor at University of Santiago, Chile, combining it with writing fiction.

**Ava Kadishson Schieber**'s work is influenced by her memories of the Holocaust and her experiences as a survivor. Born in

Novi Sad in the former Yugoslavia, her family was relatively successful and comfortable until the arrival of the Nazis. Ignoring the Nazis' mandate that all Jewish families register as such, her family decided to split up and go into hiding. At the time fifteen years old, Schieber spent four years pretending to be deaf and mute as she hid on a remote Serbian farm. Despite her dire circumstances, she kept making art during this period, and one of the watercolors that she painted during this time can be found in the US Holocaust Museum. After the war, she discovered that her father and sister had been killed. She reunited with her mother and the two initially lived in Yugoslavia before emigrating to Israel in 1949, where Kadishson Schieber met her husband. The pair worked together at an improv theater in Tel Aviv, and she began to paint and collect artifacts. After her husband's death in the early 1980s, Kadishson Schieber began exhibiting her work in the United States and eventually moved to Chicago where she lived with her second husband until her death in 2022.

**Entela Kasi** is the current Albanian PEN President and serves as Ambassador for Peace. A poet, novelist, translator, and essayist, her presence resonates significantly within the cultural realm of Albania, where she is recognized as a prominent intellectual. Her engagement in the realm of ideas is not limited to her creative writing alone, as she regularly contributes to Albanian journals and daily press, often delving into topics surrounding social movements, culture, and politics. She has been translated into, among others, Macedonian, Serbian, Turkish, Bulgarian, Romanian, Italian, German, French, English, Hebrew. She writes in both Albanian and English.

**Gordana Kuić** was a Serbian novelist. She graduated in English Language and Literature from the University of Belgrade and worked at the American Embassy in Belgrade and the Soros Foundation in New York. She is the award-winning author of nine best-selling novels as well as two books of short stories. Kuić is the winner of the prestigious Women's Pen Prize (Zlatno Pero), five Golden Best-Sellers, and two Belgrade Book Fair Prizes. She is a prolific author, whose works have repeatedly been adapted both for the stage (including ballet adaptations) and the screen, most notably *The Scent of Rain in the Balkans* and *The Blossom of Linden in the Balkans*, both of which became widely successful television series on the National Broadcasting Service in Serbia. Her work has been translated into numerous languages, including English and Hebrew, while in Serbian she remains one of the most widely read contemporary authors. Topics relevant to her work are the destinies of various Jewish communities in the Balkans in the nineteenth and twentieth centuries.

**Luljeta Lleshanaku** is a highly acclaimed poet, born in Elbasan, Albania. Known for her introspective and philosophical poetry, Leshanaku has made significant contributions to contemporary Albanian literature. Lleshanaku was raised under the Stalinist regime of Enver Hoxha, where she was prevented from pursuing an education the way she would have liked. Lleshanaku's poetry is characterized by its precise and concise language. She is the recipient of prestigious awards, including the Crystal Vilenica Award. Her poems have been translated into numerous languages, cementing her status as a celebrated representative of Albanian literature on the global stage.

**Myriam Moscona** is a Mexican-born journalist, poet, and translator from a Bulgarian Sephardic family. She has published eleven books of poetry, including *Las visitantes* (1989), *Vísperas* (1996), *Negro marfil* (2006), *Ansina* (2015), and most recently *La muerte de la lengua inglesa* (2021). In addition to these works, she has also published a novel in Judeo-Spanish entitled *Tela de sevoya* (2012), as well as a collection of literary portraits and interviews and an anthology of works in Ladino by other members of the Sephardic diaspora. Across her diverse publications, the motifs of displacement and memory appear – especially with respect to the history and expcriences of the Sephardic diaspora. Moscona's works have been translated into several languages. She has also won various awards, including the Aguascalientes National Poetry Award in 1998 and the Guggenheim Fellowship in 2006. She currently lives in Mexico City.

**Angelina Muñiz Huberman** is a Mexican writer, poet, and professor whose works frequently explore Sephardic history and crypto-Judaism. She was born in France to parents who had fled the Spanish Civil War but her family, following the Nazi advance on France, subsequently fled to Cuba in 1939 and then to Mexico City in 1942. When she was six, she discovered her Sephardic ancestry. This discovery inspired her to convert to Judaism and fueled her accomplished career. She has written nearly 50 books, including *Morada interior* (1972), *Dulcinea encantada* (1992), *El siglo del desencanto* (2002), and *El sefardí romántico* (2014). In 2021, she was inducted into the Mexican Academy of Language – the country's most prestigious literary body – and in 2022, she received an honorary doctorate from the National Autonomous University of Mexico.

**Rosa Nissàn** is a Mexican writer of Sephardic origin. She is known for her literary works that seek to restore a female perspective to the official national story of Mexico – specifically concerning a unique and often overlooked group: the Mexican-Sephardic. It is Nissán's own experiences and expertise as a Mexican woman of Sephardic heritage that inspires and shapes her works. Her books tell the stories of individuals left out of the national narrative, thereby (re)inserting them into the collective memory and by examining Jewish culture alongside or as a part of Mexican culture, she recuperates the Sephardic tradition within its Mexican frame. Her unique voice and approach to literature have facilitated an accomplished career, with the Ariel León Dultzin Award from the Association of Israeli Journalists and Writers in Mexico in 1994. Currently, Nissán lives in Mexico City, where she continues to engage in various literary activities.

**Michèle Sarde** was born in Brittany, France, just after the start of World War II. Both her parents were of Judeo-Hispanic stock whose families migrated to France in the 1920s. Her mother's family came from Salonica and her father's from Burgas, Bulgaria, and from Constanţa, Romania, all formerly Ottoman territories. As a child, Michèle lived in hiding under the German occupation. After the war, she grew up in Paris and studied literature at the Sorbonne. She moved to the United States in 1969, where she taught French literature and culture, together with gender and intercultural studies at Georgetown University. In 2000, now a Professor Emerita, she moved to Chile and now devotes herself to writing. Her literary work is cross-cultural and cross-disciplinary and reflects this experience at the intersection between three of the world's regions. The key themes of her work, for which she has won literary awards, are the observation of women, intercultural issues, the interaction between history and individual destinies and twentieth-century totalitarian systems, and the interweaving of personal and historical memory. Her books have been translated into Dutch, English, Italian, Japanese, Spanish and Russian. She holds the *Palmes académiques*, the Order of Arts and Letters, and the Order of National Merit, awarded by the French Government. She has written biographies of the women writers Colette and Marguerite Yourcenar, a biography of the Franco-Polish writer Jacques Rossi, who survived nineteen years in the Soviet Gulag, as well as two volumes on the history and sociology of women in France.

# Copyright

Rosa Nissán, "May You Make a Good Bride". Excerpt from *Like a Bride/Novia que te vea*, Feminist Press, 2020. Translated from the Spanish by Dina Castillo-Mendoza.

Myriam Moscona, "Windmill". From the collection entitled *Tela de Sevoya (Onioncloth)*, Les Figues Press, 2017. Translated from the Spanish by Celeste Kostopulos-Cooperman.

Gordana Kuić, "Chapter I: Sarajevo, 1914". Excerpt from *The Scent of Rain in the Balkans*, Alnari/Vulkan izdavaštvo, 2010. Translated from the Serbian by Richard Williams.

Ava Kadishson Schieber, "Farewell". *Soundless Roar: Stories, Poems, and Drawings*, Northwestern University Press, 2002.

Ruth Behar, "Remembering Silivri at Hotel Majestic". Copyright of the author.

Michèle Sarde, "In Search of Marie J". Copyright of the author. Translated from the French by Domnica Radulescu.

Andrea Jeftanovic, "Sarajevo Underground". *Errant Destinations*, Lexington Books, 2024. Translated from the Spanish by Jacqueline C. Nanfito.

Angelina Muñiz Huberman, "The Portuguese Synagogue". *The House of Memory* (edited by Marjorie Agosín), Solis Press, 2022. Translated from the Spanish by Martha Manier.

Mimoza Erebara, "Jerusalem Is a City on a Hill". Copyright of the author. Translated from the Albanian by Halil Bashota.

Luljeta Lleshanaku, "Prisoners", "Old People's House". Copyright of the author. Translated from the Albanian by Halil Bashota.

Entela Kasi, "Amidah: The Silent Prayer". Copyright of the author. Translated from the Albanian by Halil Bashota.

Rita Gabbai-Simantov, "Silence", "Pretty Salonican Girls". Copyright: Shmuel Refael, *Un grito en el silencio. La poesía sobre el Holocausto en lengua sefardí: Estudio y Antología*, 1ª edición en español, Tirocinio S.L. 2008.

Michal Held Delaroza, "In the End What Remains Are the Words: A Late Letter to My Grandmother Sali". Copyright of the author.

www.ingramcontent.com/pod-product-compliance
Lightning Source LLC
Chambersburg PA
CBHW061232070526
44584CB00030B/4093